JOHNNY HANDLE
Life and Soul

Pete Wood

ISBN 978-0-9576187-9-4

First published in England in 2017 by Pete Wood

Printed and bound by
Martins the Printers Limited
Seaview Works, Spittal
Berwick-upon-Tweed, TD15 1RS
www.martins-the-printers.com

Set in 11.75/15 Century Old Style
Design by www.simprimstudio.com

Contents

Acknowledgements and preface

I wish to thank all those who have helped me to produce this biography. Most important has been Johnny himself, who has entertained us both during twelve interviews and other conversations between January 2016 and April 2017. These sessions, largely a series of stories, some relevant, some tangential, have been highly entertaining for me, and though I thought I knew him well, I have discovered other aspects of his life and career, many of which have been included in the book! Also interviewed have been Alistair Anderson, John Brennan, Ron Duke, John Gall, Vic Gammon, Tom Gilfellon, Benny Graham, Dave Harker, Christine Hendry, Gary Hogg, Dave Normanton, Brian Pandrich, Ed Pickford, Colin Ross, Ray Shenton, and Mike Tickell. Others who have contributed include Jim Bainbridge, Pete Coe and Jim Mageean. I wish to thank Brian Shuel for the cover photograph of Johnny in younger days, the main image on the front cover and also found inside, and his photograph of him with others at Keele Folk Festival in 1966. Johnny has been very active in the construction of the book, and whilst being the most acute and helpful of editors, has been unable to resist the temptation to attenuate reports of some of his excesses. Some of these, on and off the stage, whilst having caused great hilarity with audiences, may have obscured his many important contributions to the second folk revival, and to North East culture.

I published a biography of the Elliotts of Birtley in 2008, which was the result of my astonishment that nobody else had done this. The book was a success, and several people afterwards would approach me with the question "Why not do a book about Johnny Handle?" Well, I thought he definitely merited a biography, but resisted because I was busy with other projects, and thought I was too close to the subject. However, at New Year 2016, I was finally convinced by a friend and connoisseur of North East culture that it was a project long overdue. Indeed it is, and I can only hope that I have done him credit.

This book is a biography rather than an academic exercise, and only sufficient references are included to guide the interested reader to relevant original sources. Johnny's musical creations and recordings are so many that although selections of the former are considered in Chapters 7 to 9, and key albums are considered, readers in search of more detail should consult his website, where comprehensive lists of his achievements can be found.

www.johnnyhandle.co.uk

Pete Wood
Summer 2017

Prologue

IN EARLY 1958, JOHNNY HANDLE, A JAZZ PLAYER IN HIS EARLY TWENTIES, HAD A regular spot at the New Orleans Jazz Club in Newcastle. The skiffle craze of 1956 had led to great interest in American songs, especially the blues, with American stars making regular appearances in the UK. So Johnny was doing Big Bill Broonzy numbers, aided by a 4-string guitar tuned like a banjo, one of many instruments he had already learnt to play. One night, another man showed up who was also doing blues. As Johnny memorably puts it: "This chap from Oxford appears. He was a better singer and better guitar player than I was, so I ups and says 'Whee are ye like?'". The "chap from Oxford" was Gateshead-born and bred Louis Killen, who was definitely not from Oxford. He was a regular Geordie in fact, who had had a job as a carpenter in the reconstruction of one of the Oxford colleges. While "doon sooth", he had had guitar lessons from none other than Alexis Korner, probably the best blues guitarist in the country at that time. The night was a Thursday in February 1958, celebrated as the start of the first folk club in the North East, Folksong and Ballad.

In fact the "folk proper" did not start for a few months. Less than a month after this meeting, Johnny was away on holiday, and Louis assumed his spot at the club. I'd have given a great deal to be there the week Johnny returned, when "discussions ensued". Fortunately, they agreed to share the spot, and as Louis once put it to me: "We became the Sonny and Brownie of the North". The first number was *Mother's not dead* with Johnny on banjo, and Louis on guitar. This arrangement carried on for a few months, eventually becoming a whole night of singing, as opposed to jazz. They continued doing a lot of blues, Woody Guthrie songs, and Jimmy Rodgers yodelling, but with floor singers like the Irish oriented John Reavey, this inevitably extended to things we would call folk songs, and increasingly non-American ones.

Louis' time down south had not only helped make him a very good blues guitarist, but had brought him into contact with British folk music by attending the Heritage Society nights in Oxford, and the folk clubs in London then operated by Ewan McColl. He was also influenced by a Manchester man, Brian Ballinger, who was a regular at the first folk club in the country, started by Harry Boardman in 1954. So much so that Brian told Louis "It's your duty to start a club like Harry". At some time, Louis said to Johnny: "Ye're singing like an American but you're talkin' like a Geordie". This sort of directness was typical of what was to be a lifelong relationship (says Johnny "He was always bossy"). But the comment was remarkably prescient in view of what was to come.

Chapter 1. Childhood, the War, and early music

"I have few facts, mostly memory"

JOHNNY'S FULL NAME IS JOHN ALAN PANDRICH, AND WE WILL SEE A LITTLE LATER how he got the name which he has had most of his life. Born in 1935, the first five years of his life were spent in Walkerville, in east Newcastle. Walker, though now described as residential, had been a heavily industrialised area with pits, and Armstrong's engineering works. Walkerville was a slightly more refined area, in keeping with his father's job, that of a schoolteacher. His father had been educated at the best school in the city, Royal Grammar School (RGS), and had first worked as an industrial chemist. However, he quickly spotted that people were being paid off, and saw the need to do something else. Johnny's paternal grandfather had been a printer from Dundee, who had come down to Newcastle to work for Mawson Swan and Morgan as a compositor, and at this time was able to find the money for him to train as a teacher. His first job was in the west end of Newcastle, but he moved to Walkerville for a better-paid job. So Johnny was basically a middle class lad living in a working class area.

His parents were also teetotal and churchgoers, a notable contrast to his own later lifestyle. This most likely reflected the changing times between the thirties and the fifties, but could also be some sort of social reaction by him. Like most of us, he does not remember much of his very early days, but maybe what he does remember is significant. His mother's family had relatives in Yorkshire, and late in 1939, she took him on a long train journey to her family in Pateley Bridge with a view to his evacuation in the event of war. So, little John aged four, remembers the dogs and watering the animals on the farm. This presaged a rural early childhood, which whilst being brought about by World War II, was somewhat idyllic. His maternal grandfather had come from Yorkshire, became a horseman and eventually head groom to the agent of several

Washington collieries. When he retired, his family had clubbed together to get a house just outside Morpeth, near to the golf course. Which is where the five-year-old Alan was dispatched for the first six months of the war. He remembers the trains going past the house towards Rothbury, and his granddad keeping canaries and rabbits on his allotment beyond the railway. Just imagine the thrill this young lad from the "toon" got from finding this freedom "outbye". But it was elsewhere that he was to spend the rest of the war years. [For foreigners, "the toon" is central Newcastle; "outbye" means far away, up-country, but is also used to mean leaving somewhere, as in "coming outbye"; "canny" has lots of meanings.]

It is hardly surprising that arrangements for evacuating children from the big cities to the countryside were somewhat chaotic, and Johnny's father became involved in protracted negotiations to move his school from Walkerville to Beaufront Castle just outside Hexham. (This chateau-like building is still standing, privately owned, in an imposing position above the A69 between Corbridge and Hexham). Johnny stayed with his mum in a cottage about half a mile away from the castle, from 1940 to 1944. He had to be "schooled" of course, so attended the local school at Beaufront. He remembers the headmistress, a formidable woman who had deigned to visit the cottage one day for cucumber sandwiches to make the arrangements. It was at this school that he heard the "bus to Morpeth", a mile away, grinding the gears as it struggled up Oakwood Bank. This was much later commemorated by fellow songwriter Terry Conway in his hilarious eponymous song.

It is clear that the young lad was fascinated by what he saw around him. When I asked him about this, aged 81, he started drawing a map of the immediate area, and got lyrical about the various workers on the estate. The farm was of course managed mostly by horses, with maybe just the one old tractor. In those days, there was no Health and Safety, so as a child you'd wander around talking to these old boys, and absorbing what they were doing. I remember doing something similar, working on a local farm, for nowt, just enjoying the various jobs, such as driving the tractor with the buckrake on the back, ferrying grass to the silage pit, and stomping on the independent brakes to turn the whole thing up in the air.

Beaufront was when he first heard local music. At the village school, he tells me that there was country dancing, with some songs. His Aunties (Lucy, Bessy, and Winnie) came out from the town from time to time, often staying over to escape the bombing. He remembers the austere evenings with tea and cakes and the Aunties going to church. He a reluctant participant, bored at walking behind the others as they strolled down to Oakwood and on to the hamlet of St. John Lee, the nearest church. But by 1943, aged eight, he had started taking piano lessons, and would often be invited to do a party piece, before being packed off to bed with a candle. He was not happy with this, of course, especially with "all the spiders which gathered round the candle". (The house was lit by candles and oil lamps, normal in country areas in those days. In town, houses had electricity, following on from gas – he mentioned seeing gas mantles at a relative's house in Stanhope Street in Newcastle. (I remember them at my granny's and my Aunty Janet's house in Woodland Road, Gorton, as late as the fifties.)

Meanwhile, downstairs, they would "get the teapot out and father and mother would play hymns on the piano". But then they would sing "Catcheside Warrington songs" which he listened to intently[1]. Suddenly, a pious evening had become *Hey wor Nanny's a 'mazor.*[2] Much, much more interesting of course, to a lad of almost any age. The family, in their soiree, had of course put on the accent, reading the odd dialect words under the music! But the young Johnny was hearing was the Northumbrian accent from the people around Beaufront. The Tyneside songs were "in an alien tongue", because it seems universal that the city accent is quite different from that of the surrounding countryside. (The Manchester accent is markedly different from the Lancashire accent, so it is probably a widespread characteristic.) So,

---

1 Catcheside Warrington was an Edwardian music hall performer and prolific early recording artist, concentrating on Geordie material. These songs were composed by the local writers such as Ned Corvan, George Ridley, Joe Wilson, and latterly Tommy Armstrong. Four volumes of *Tyneside* Songs were published starting in 1912, with not only all the words, but the dots as well. These were the days when the piano was at its height, when many ordinary working class houses would have one. The books were very important in conserving this aspect of Geordie culture in the musical "dark days" of the 30s and 40s when American songs tended to predominate

2 One of Tommy Armstrong's songs about a hilarious day out of real working class people.

Pandrich Family, early fifties. Johnny at left, Brian in front, Father second right, middle row. Uncle George at extreme right

although Johnny talks with a definite Newcastle accent, he slips easily into the dialect more associated with rural Northumberland.

Eventually, Johnny's dad's pupils drifted back to their homes and schools in the town. He carried on at the local school with the remaining town kids, but then Newcastle council said he had to go back to teach in town, so he spent the weekends and holidays with Johnny and mum at the cottage. He would commute on the Wrights bus, a service still running between Newcastle and Keswick[3].

Towards the end of the war, Johnny would occasionally visit his dad in town and they went fire watching in the towers at Westgate Hill School, built to look like a Scottish castle. From there, of course, they could see across the city. He does not remember anything exciting

3 Wright Bros buses, based in Nenthead at the head of Weardale, have been running since just after World War one, is still family owned, and is famous amongst the older members of the population for running services other operators shun. The 888, from Newcastle to Keswick, is reputed to be the most scenic bus drive in England, going over Hartside Pass, regularly blocked by snow drifts (in the days of proper winters!). It had to compete with the railways when it started, but on closure of the line in 1972, the bus has had the monopoly. In the 1970s, it started the "Alston Garrigill circular", a triumph of hope over experience, surely. I could go on!

happening, but one night the incendiary bombs destroyed his granny's house. Fortunately, she was out visiting George, her son. He worked for Burton the Tailor of immaculate dress fame, and was a musician. He had a band, lived near Chillingham Road, and regularly played at the Heaton Electric, a local cinema and entertainment venue. According to Johnny, he was making more money out of music than the day job, a feat he was later to emulate. At family gatherings, they'd all "get up and play the piano a bit, as well as singing Tyneside songs, but George would play the thirties standards". Whereas Dad was "a fairly inaccurate piano player", who could manage school assemblies, brother George could really play. "I got to know a lot more about Uncle George through visiting him at the old people's home at Whitley Bay, when he enjoyed talking about the music scene in the thirties. He took his small electric organ with him to the home. Dad was in the same home, and together with George's banjo player from the thirties we made quite a nuisance of ourselves having afternoon sessions, with accordion, organ, piano and banjo. The old ladies who were nominally crotcheting, but actually sleeping the afternoon away, complained about being kept awake!"

The young Johnny was a somewhat capricious music student. At Beaufront, his parents found he didn't "come through" his piano lessons, i.e. he didn't take grades, not because of lack of keyboard ability, but because he had difficulty reading music. At lessons, he would play *Für Elise* (didn't we all?), but the teacher would criticise him because he was learning it by ear, and not by the dots. (The giveaway was that he would carry on playing without turning the music over). However, when he took lessons at Oakwood with Mr Morrow he would say "You're going to get somewhere with this". Johnny gave up lessons himself aged eleven or twelve when he started thinking "this is too slow, this music thing, it's a waste of time, I can pick out the tunes from the wireless." He mentions Charlie Kunz, whose records my parents had had since the thirties. "It seemed so simple what he was doing." He noticed the chord progressions, and how it could be applied to anything (this is not the stuff of piano grades). "It was fairly straightforward to work out how the chords changed. So that was the beginning. I could soak it up".

In 1945, aged ten, after some coaching by his dad, he got a scholarship to Heaton Grammar School. Then, in his early teenage years, he would continue to "pick up stuff from the wireless". By the age of thirteen, he was going to the church youth club, which used to organise swaps with other youth clubs, where he became quite popular as a piano player. He was suddenly in demand. (He describes it as "equivalent to his first gig".) On these occasions, he'd be playing for up to ninety minutes, ("I was up for that"), and went down very well, playing standards like *Sunny Side Of The Street* and *Georgia*, and playing for the dance. "The youth club had young ladies and a piano, so I would play it." And these teenagers would dance to the piano. Clearly he was "scoring" in more senses than one, but there was a girl called Joyce, who was better than him. "I thought, I'm not goin to have this". He decided to "practise and practise" till he was better than her, which he duly did. This was an early sign of his competitiveness, which he cannot resist. He describes himself at this time as "having an adolescent surge, needing to impress, to make a mark. I was not a leader of the pack socially, bit out of it". The term "introvert" starts briefly to come to mind, until you think about what he was to become. He says "Sometimes you need to be extrovert in order to gain some confidence". Sure he wanted to be wanted – I say it's normal. Later in his teens he mixed with the mad pack, people who took the mickey out of teachers, but he also mentioned some teachers of a quality he would respect, his highest praise being expressed as "I will graft for him".

Another feature of the fifties important in Johnny's life was the goon show. His crazy humour on and off stage, and the characters he invented like Genghis Sprott, are a testament to this. At Heaton Grammar he was the leader of what he calls "an anorak group of our own", which acted out the recent edition of the goons, and whose humour sometimes spread to the rest of the class. The English teacher would often bear the brunt of this. He was something of an eccentric, and having been in the army during the war continued to wear ex-army clothes, including army socks held up by suspenders! No wonder they took the mickey. Johnny was nagged by the teachers, "You've got to get those O levels boy", but the attractions of the jazz world overcame this. He felt a touch of sympathy for some teachers, since ex-army staff who had taken a crash teaching course following the war were looked down on by the regular teachers, who wore a gown, which the newcomers were not allowed. This shows an amazing insight into his mentors, in keeping with his obvious intelligence. Johnny and I have parallel experiences regarding grammar schools. Having been outstanding in my primary school, I got special lessons along with two other boys and two girls to take separate exams for Direct Entrance schools in Manchester. Having passed these exams, I went to Manchester Grammar School, to find myself in Form 1D, meaning there were at least 70 boys cleverer than myself. A humbling experience, which Johnny had undergone some eight years earlier at Heaton Grammar. I have to admit that he climbed the academic ladder faster than me, but his attitude was definitely anti-establishment. Having passed the first few years of his life in rural Northumberland, listening to the broad accents of the people out there, he found the clipped accents of the grammar school somewhat stifling, where much prominence was given to producing a Gilbert and Sullivan opera every year, academic achievement, and sport.

Chapter 2. Jazz Days

"Aa could have taken the blues route like Alan Price but I never had the get up and go"

MUSICALLY, IN THE LATE 1940S, HE WAS NOTABLY "VEERING TOWARDS IT" i.e. jazz, particularly Sid Phillips and Freddie Randall. "I couldn't work out what made them tick at first, but then realised it was the quality of the improvisation, compared with other bands that were playing off the dots." At school, he remembers listening to a radio programme of jazz, at four in the afternoon (surely somewhat avant-garde for those times?). A lot of the pop music was "a bit baynell" (banal – he takes great delight in deliberately mispronouncing what he regards as highfalutin words). With jazz "you could escape from the dots" However, he did not like the lack of structure in modern jazz. Dixieland musicians like Bix Beiderbeck were "trapped into playing for the dance, but after would go back and jam". He sees this as similar to his later playing for ceilidhs. (He is constantly projecting forwards from his jazz days to his later folk days.) Having borrowed a guitar at fourteen "as a recreational thing", he and a mate, Don, who was into Django Reinhardt, walked the Maiden's Way, an old Roman road from Corbridge to Holy Island. They were aged about fifteen, carrying both camping gear and guitars, and he remembers the day they went into the Fox and Hounds, a pub on Stagshaw Bank, where they entertained the whole pub for an hour or so. *Big Rock Candy Mountain* and *Down by the riverside* were typical of what they played.

As mentioned in the previous chapter, Johnny had started hostelling in his early teens, which is how, in about 1950, he met a clarinet player called Colin Beale. Colin was a keen cyclist, who could on occasion do 120 miles a day. Cycling was then at its height, when Sunday mornings would find several groups starting at various points of the Great North Road in the town. He and Johnny would go hostelling most weekends, and they had discovered the Rye Hill Youth Club in the west end of Newcastle, which became a place where cyclists and hostellers went on Sunday night, after the day's exertions. "All the crack was there. The Elswick kids came as well, they didn't go hostelling, but it was their club, and they had a resident band. So, on Sunday night it was the hikers, me and Colin, and the band. Naturally, we joined in, me on piano and Colin on clarinet. The band would copy Lyttleton and Armstrong records exactly." By now Johnny was sixteen, taking O levels, about to go into the sixth form, and a school jazz band was formed, naturally including him on piano. He was already doing some other gigs with Colin Beale, all of which was giving him a great experience. For his sixteenth birthday he got a new guitar from his dad, a conventional six-string, as opposed to the famous 4-string which we'll look at later. The school band ran until the end of 1951, until various people left school. But Johnny was already exploring the jazz scene outside school and the youth club. Of this period, he says "I have few facts, mostly memory", but let us try and piece this stuff together into some kind of chronology.

A man who was to become one of the most influential jazz musicians in the area, Clem Avery, was playing piano with the Louisana Jazz Band on Sunday lunchtimes at Blaydon Conservative Club (note!), and Johnny started going there regularly. When Clem left, Johnny took his place on piano, playing from 1952 to 1953. Meanwhile, Clem had started his own band, The Clem Avery Jazzmen, where he was now playing trumpet. They had searched for pubs without success, and had finished up at a gentleman's club in Heaton, the Alexander Club. Johnny played piano with him from 1953 to 1954. The Avery band had a great repertoire, with all the classics of Louis Armstrong and Jelly Roll Morton, which they learnt off 78rpm records. 1954 saw jazz starting at the Royal Arcade in the city centre. In 1955, Clem went to do national service in the RAF, and banjo player Joe Young took over at the Royal Arcade, re-christening himself as "Mighty Joe".

In 1955 he acquired several instruments. The first was the cornet which he bought in a junk shop. It needed thirty-odd soldered patches, which of course he did himself, and he sat in on it with several jazz bands. He soon moved on to the trumpet, which he says requires more skill, and tells the tale of playing with Mighty Joe on second trumpet. This he had done after a mere four lessons on the instrument! (He thought this was normal, a recognisable characteristic of his modesty.) However, he got disillusioned when the band moved into the reviled mainstream repertoire, and so he set up his own band. (It may also be something to with playing **second** trumpet). He needed a bass player, so Johnny bought a three-stringed instrument (his sister called it Nicodemus, which I've yet to fathom). In the band, it was played by David Reed, a banjo player. The band was called The Levee Ramblers, but didn't last long.

Lastly that year he picked up the banjo, an essential requirement of any traditional jazz band of course, and later it came in handy in the skiffle craze of 1956 and 1957. "There were lots of skiffle groups, every office in town had one. Lots of guitars, of course, but the groups needed a different sound, and I found the banjo easier than the guitar". He later adapted the guitar to have four strings tuned like a banjo, and became famous for this in the folk movement. In 1956, on his 21st birthday, he was playing at the Jesmond Co-op Hall with Colin Beale, when Colin lent him a tenor saxophone. His comments on this are laconic "If you play only a few tunes, you can sound quite good." Yes, he could play it now, if required (as with most instruments). Yet another instrument introduced to him by Colin was the euphonium. Colin was playing the clarinet in the Territorial Army Band, reckoning that you got a better deal on national service, and was playing all over the place. He tried to get Johnny interested in joining as a third euphonium player. "Third euph player doesn't need much intelligence. It's like a melodeon player with one row. You just sort of blow it and twiddle it, and busk along". Unfortunately for him there came an occasion when the other two failed to turn up. His busking was revealed, and he got the sack. Good to know he's human, and not good at everything. Later, another euphonium came in handy when recording the LP *Canny Newcassel* in 1972, where Colin Ross used it to accompany *The fire on the quay*. (Johnny has lost his copy, but has just bought a one off the web for £15!) It was also used to vent his spleen on being woken by the cathedral bells on a Sunday morning. He waited till the bells had stopped and "the churchgoers were praying", opened a window, and played the euphonium as hard as possible over and over again.

Ray Shenton, now a distinguished jazz pianist, heard his first jazz band at Gosforth in 1954, with Johnny on piano. Even then Ray says, he had a unique style, vamping four to the bar with the left hand, with the right hand accompanying with chords. Ray was also impressed by Johnny's 4-string guitar style, already mentioned, and by the sheer number of tunes he knew. "He must have had an enormous number of records" (not sure this is true-he listened to a lot of wireless). Johnny was very highly regarded by the jazzers. "He gave the folk scene a shot in the arm when be branched out into this genre." Ray formed the River City Jazzmen, who did their own thing for many years. It's good to see that in recent years the two old jazzers have become re-acquainted by appearing at a regular afternoon session of humour and music at Dave Normanton's zany afternoon at South Gosforth once a month. Ray's band had a double bass, and as none of them had cars in those days, it presented some transport problems. "We used to have to wait for a particular trolley bus where you could fit it into the space". Johnny says he had a similar problem, having to wait for a bus with a spiral staircase which the bass would fit in snugly. Dave Normanton, outstanding MC and entertainer, tells a great story concerning the double bass. One Christmas he was out playing with Johnny at The Golden Lion in Winlaton Mill, known as Danny's pub by the locals, and celebrated in song by Johnny as we shall see later. After the gig, they had to get the bass up the hill to Johnny's house. So, here's Normanton holding the pointy end, with Johnny on the scroll end. It's snowing, and they are passing the bus queue who have just emerged from the social club opposite Danny's. Johnny just couldn't resist it. As they passed the queue, he started plucking out *Mary's Boy Child* on the by now horizontal strings of the bass. They got a huge round of applause. I would love to have been there. Nowadays, somebody would have videoed it on the phone. Maybe it's better to use your imagination.

Meanwhile, the jazz fraternity was having difficulties finding venues, a lot of pubs regarding these young men as "undesirable", so a co-operative was established to set up a jazz club in a rundown social club in Melbourne Street, Shieldfield, a shabby inner city area. A bank loan was arranged, repairs and improvements made, and they opened as the New Orleans Club in 1955. Vieux Carreé were the resident band there, supported by others, and the club eventually had jazz seven days a week. Part of the stimulus for him learning so many instruments was National Service, where men of eighteen had to do two years in the forces,

DANCE ON: A typical crowded scene with the band blasting out their music at the New Orleans Jazz Club in Newcastle

Jiving to the band at the New Orleans Club, late fifties. Johnny on double bass, top left.

regarded by many as wasting time. So Johnny, who was at this time employed in the pits, making him exempt from this iniquity, would leap into any vacancy thus created, even if it meant learning a completely new instrument. Banjo-trumpet-guitar-double bass-piano, he could fit into "a variety of situations". By 1957, he was a regular in the Vieux Carreé band on bass, the beauty of which was that the instrument was stored permanently at the New Orleans club, so Johnny started playing every Friday and Sunday for a bottle of amber (the club had debts to repay).

Johnny had left Heaton Grammar at seventeen to work at Dudley colliery as what is known as a "datal hand", a worker who was not on piecework, but he was also doing qualifications at college by day release, and by the time the folk club started, he was a qualified mine surveyor, notably at the Rising Sun Colliery at Wallsend. Not only was he getting "tickets", he was experiencing all aspects of life down the pit, which he was to incorporate so vividly in the songs he wrote just a little while later, and just as importantly speaking with knowledge about so many aspects of "pitmatic" culture.

Brian Pandrich, Johnny's younger brother by eight years, shared a bedroom with the teenage Johnny, and remembers the jazz player at home. Brian was used at first as a "gopher", for instance when the family

Johnny at the Rising Sun Colliery

rented a Whitley Bay bungalow for a holiday, Johnny would camp some distance along the coast, with Brian ferrying messages between them. At home, Johnny would get up for pit at five am, and immediately start playing the recording he'd made on a tape recorder the night before. It could be the goon show, or a programme of ragtime. One tune was so complex that Johnny worked out that it could not be done with two hands. "They must have used a roller piano." Significantly, Brian cannot recall him actually practising, except when he was on the "crash course" on trumpet, when neighbours from two streets away complained. Johnny encouraged Brian to play guitar when he was about twelve or thirteen, and he later joined Johnny's skiffle group (Although Brian was learning the violin, in those days he felt uneasy about playing it in public. Thank heavens times have changed.) Despite Brian being famous for his "po-face", Johnny describes him as a quiet raver, and illustrates this by a story about taking him home rather drunk. "Mother, this boy has been drinking" says the imperious father. I feel sure that Brian's po-face was in order to compensate for Johnny's extrovert ramblings, especially when they were playing together. He is a very talented musician, and there's more about him later in the book.

Meanwhile, Johnny had an insatiable appetite for lots of things. He liked geology, being excited about rocks and minerals, especially those in Weardale. He wanted to go to the Camborne School of Mines, but could not afford it. In Weardale camping with mates, he talked about panning for gold, and they thought he was mad. But so determined was he that he hitch-hiked all the way to one of the few gold mines in Britain, Dolgelly in North Wales (he always did thorough research). "It rained the whole time, no panning was done, I nearly fell off Cader Idris, and so came back goldless". His mates started to call him Panhandle (because of Pandrich), and when he played with the school Jazz Band, they just called him Handle. He didn't like "Alan", as his parents always called him, and so the legend was born. Johnny Handle he was called for evermore. Many years later, he took two of his young children, Megan and Matty, down a gold mine. As with everything he enthuses about, he gave me much detail about panning.

The late fifties was, of course, the time of the skiffle craze, which had emerged from traditional jazz bands, led by Lonnie Donegan, who had started out playing banjo in Chris Barber's Band, one of the leading traditional jazz bands nationally. Skiffle was a souped-up form of American folk songs, which only needed one singer and an acoustic guitar. Guess who fitted this role on Tyneside in the mid-fifties? Yes, it was Johnny Handle, who as well as playing bass in the Vieux Carreé Band, was now doing an interval spot of largely skiffle and blues. The story of the making of the Animals' version of *The house of the rising sun* is now well known, but Eric Burdon's source is not often included. Burdon was singing in various jazz clubs during the fifties, and revealed that he first heard the song "in a club in Newcastle, where it was sung by a Northumbrian folk singer called Johnny Handle". And in a Radio Four programme in 2008 Eric came out with the immortal line in broad Geordie: "Why, we wad waak doon Pilgrim Street, and see the River Tyne, and we wad just pretend that it was the Mississippi!"

At the same time, Johnny would be looking for any musical action that could yield an income. In 1956 he worked for an agency running

Heaton Electric Palace. Uncle George had a regular spot in the thirties when it was a dance hall.

concert parties, which consisted of a male singer who crooned like Dean Martin, a female covering Doris Day (as Johnny mentions "never like Ella, sadly"), and a comic carrying the music. Although Johnny at the time could not read the dots very well, the chords were included underneath, which was all he needed to play the piano. He remembers the group meeting at the South Africa memorial in the middle of town, to go by bus to working mens' clubs in places like Bedlington, Blyth, and Ashington. Sometime later, the group had a gig at the Excelsior Club in Ashington. To Johnny's astonishment, he got a call from his Uncle Billy, saying he was the resident pianist at the club. That's a father and two uncles who were musicians! Uncle Billy was the bachelor brother of Johnny's mother, who lived with his parents just outside Morpeth where Johnny spent the first part of the war, described briefly in Chapter 1. Despite not having known about Billy's piano playing, on the night "He told me that I should immediately go upstairs and start playing. This I did, as they had just received delivery of a new grand piano. and I needed no encouragement! After hearing me play, he told me that I could 'dep' for him any time I liked! That was a real treat". He also did a two-year piano residency at Dudley Bottom Club between 1959 and 1961. This wide experience stood him in good stead after he decided that folk music was where his future lay.

Chapter 3. The early folk club 1958 to 1965

"Pitta poond, tappy lappy doon the lonnin'"

LOUIS KILLEN WAS ABOUT THE SAME AGE AS JOHNNY, WITH A GATESHEAD working class background that had been steeped in every kind of music. He'd been in the church choir, and there was singing at home. As with many other Tyneside families, the songs had a strong Irish influence, but they also did lots of the Geordie stuff from the Catcheside Warrington books. Whilst the North East has its own musical culture, this was at its nadir in the 1940s, and like the rest of the early revivalists, Louis came to folk singing via American music. One of his older brothers was a guitarist with his own dance band, and the other brought back lots of records when on leave from the Navy. These would include jazz immortals such as Charlie Parker, Stan Kenton, Pee Wee Hunt, but also country records like Grand Ol' Oprey, Roy Acuff and the Smoky Mountain Boys, and Grandpa Jones. He was very early into the fledgling Newcastle jazz scene, first going to the Newcastle Rhythm Club when he was sixteen. (This was another age, when people listened to record recitals, such as a retrospective on Louis Armstrong he remembered with particular relish.)

Louis was drifting around, having tried several "proper jobs". He was not one to settle to a career, nor did he have the discipline to complete his course at the Catholic Workers' College, but he too had discovered skiffle. He was a trained carpenter, so could get work in Oxford, where he joined in with others playing "Donegan stuff". He also spent some time in London, attending the few folk venues that were then operating. He recalled in the spring of 1957 calling on Peter Kennedy, looking for a gig, maybe at Cecil Sharp House, and was persuaded to go to Northumberland to get a song from the shepherd Alan Rogerson of Commonburn near Wooler, who gave him two of his best songs. Clearly, he was gaining knowledge of folk song as a pioneer. We saw in the prologue how Louis met Johnny, and in September 1958, the two of them started a folk night on an unused night at the jazz club. Notably on the very first night, Jack Elliott and son Pete came along, then doing a lot of Jimmy Rodgers and other American songs. Having started the night out as a "freebie", and it being popular, they decided to charge, and the numbers dropped. So, they took the very positive decision to leave the jazz club, and launch a "folk club" elsewhere. Accordingly, the two set out on the first of several notable pub crawls, to find a separate venue for the folk club.

Life at The Sink

Their choice was the Barras Bridge Hotel, a rough kind of pub known affectionately as "The Sink". This was the start of the folk club proper, recalled fondly by many people still. Johnny and Louis continued to sing a mixture of British and American songs, and there was still the robust John Reavey who had sung at the Jazz Club, with the Elliotts of Birtley as regulars. Among the singers who came along in those early days were John Brennan, the softly spoken Irish singer, a contrast to John Reavey, and Laurie Charlton, an unassuming man, who brought with him a huge knowledge of traditional songs, Scots ballads in particular. They'd also had Pete Mulligan with his "Abdul a bulbul Ameer" and funny bible stories, and Ron Duke, already famous as a fisherman, who ran the door, but didn't start singing till later. The Irish piccolo and flute player John Doonan and Northumbrian piper Forster Charlton were occasional visitors, so there was music as well as songs, though they did not at that time play as a group. Guests at the Sink included Cyril Tawney, Shirley Collins, and Rambling Jack Elliott from America.

During this time, Johnny and Louis were keen not to be repetitive, continuing to seek out new songs, and they "leaned on each other quite a bit". For instance, Johnny at that time found it difficult to read the dots (amazing for such a talented musician, but there are plenty of other examples, particularly in folk music). As a result, he could not always get a song "from off the page". So Louis used to record songs onto reel to reel tape. Johnny remembers *I drew my ship* as one of these. I was surprised to find out from him, in preparing this book, that he was learning quite a lot of traditional English songs, some the sort that Louis was singing, from the "deep south" He calls these songs "pooks of hay", a phrase found in the song *Sovay*. However, Louis had by then met Ewan MacColl at his folk clubs in London, where the thing seemed to be "sing songs from where you come from". Johnny already had the standard Geordie songs like *Cushie, Blaydon*, and *Keep your Feet still* and John Reavey and John Brennan were doing Irish songs. It seemed logical to concentrate on local songs, so he did. It so happened that Louis had got hold of Bert Lloyd's *Come all ye Bold Miners*, published in 1952. It had a very large number of mining songs from the North East (hardly surprising in retrospect since the area sings about everyday life to an amazing extent, compared with the rest of England and Wales, if not the British Isles). When he showed it to Johnny, he fell upon it like a dog at broth and has not looked back since. Later he discovered the nineteenth century publications such as John Bell's *Rhymes of Northern Bards* and Allen's *Tyneside Songs*, as well as revisiting Catcheside Warrington, and eventually came to personify the genre.

One of the most important musicians in Johnny's career was Colin Ross, the fiddler and Northumbrian piper. Although memories of the time are fading, it rather looks as though Colin first came along to the Sink with the sword dance team from Monkseaton. It was some time later that he was persuaded to become one of the residents. Certainly, during 1961 he was involved in some early albums recorded for Topic. *The Collier's Rant* was an EP with Louis, Johnny, and Colin. It was clear that the North East was already important in the fast-accelerating folk revival. In the same year, Johnny made another EP, *Stottin' Doon the Waal* which had some of his early compositions, mining songs of course.

It was early in 1960 that a young Irish lad dropped into the Sink one night. He was interested in music, mostly the big band sound, and jazz. He happened on an Irish night organised by John Doonan and John Reavey, but as the Irish teenager entered the venue that night, the first music he heard, sung in harmony and with such obvious enthusiasm by the mostly English visitors, was the chorus of Brendan Behan's *The Auld Triangle*. He was fascinated, immensely impressed and deeply moved by what he saw and heard, and from then on he lived and breathed folk music. His name was Luke Kelly, and a few years later joined the fledgling Irish international group The Dubliners. Johnny remembers: „At that time the troubles in Ireland had not escalated and there were quite a few rebel songs sung, in rather a jolly way." It is said that at the

Barras Bridge Hotel ("The sink") in 1959

close of the evening Luke alone rose to his feet as the Irish National Anthem was played.

The Sink days were very informal, with numbers building from an initial twenty in 1958 till late 1961, when the room was full every week. However, civic improvements brought about a change of premises. A long-planned building of Newcastle Civic Centre had started in 1960, and by the following year, the Sink had to make way for it. So, a second pub crawl was needed by these stalwarts. This time, the last port of call was the Liberal Club in Pilgrim Street, but "how we got the liberal club I don't know. We'd be 'quite happy', and it was a private club. But when they knew what we were about, they were very supportive." This was very late in 1961, because the first advert for the Liberal Club appeared in the Evening Chronicle on 27th December. So we can safely date the first night to be either the 28th December or the 4th January. (It has proved very difficult for me to obtain some key dates from those involved due to loss of grey cells in these octogenarians)

The Liberal Club
The seating arrangements at the Liberal club meant a more formal concert performance, and several people remember a "them and us" or "platform" which was to be a feature of the club at its later venue. Jack and Pete Elliott had been regulars since the opening night and had enjoyed the more relaxed atmosphere at the Sink. It is perhaps no coincidence that it was during this period that they started their own club in Birtley, which was very different. There everybody got a chance to sing, as they went round the room, a singaround in fact. This included the other Elliotts, who had not been heard outside the family kitchen. Thus the "Elliotts of Birtley" were born, the irony of this being that their first booking was in 1962 at the Liberal Club! One of the Birtley originals, Ed Pickford, attended this evening. He remembers the Liberal Club as "a rambling old-fashioned place where the waiters wore Basil Brush waistcoats. There must have been at least nine Elliotts, up on the stage in a line like the last supper, with Jack doing most of the songs and the rest perhaps one each."

However, this was about the time that Johnny spent several months on Teesside working for ICI, sensing that the pits were on the decline. The period also coincided with the club being at the Liberal Club, and he became a fully committed "folkie", starting the Stockton folk club with songwriter Graeme Miles, and continuing to learn many new songs, including by now some written by himself. However, the job did not last long, and he needed a new one. There were now even more redundant mine surveyors than before, so he started studying for Royal Institute of Charted Surveyors exams, but quickly withdrew when he realised it would take seven years via the part-time route. He applied for lots of jobs, ranging from gold mines in Rhodesia to railway electrification on the west coast line to Scotland. Despite receiving many offers, his attachment to the local area meant he opted for Ellington pit, a modern mine working six miles out to sea.

This was late in 1962, about the time the folk club had to move again, the Liberal Club being threatened with the same fate as The Sink. So, Johnny and Louis set out on their third crusade, another pub crawl. Things were a little easier this time, as John Reavey and some Irish pals had got in with the ultimate Irish exile, Paddy Foley, landlord of the Bridge Hotel at the Newcastle side of the High Level Bridge. Said landlord was very keen on Irish rebel songs, so Reavey obliged on occasions. In the end, the Liberal Club was not demolished, but Johnny and Louis saw the attractions of Paddy Foley's and moved the club there, which is where it remained until the early 90s, when a successor club was set up at the Bridge, and still runs on a Monday night.

So, he was back on Tyneside, committed to the folk revival which was on the rise all over the country, and he had a reasonably well-paid job. However, he was only too aware of the coalfield shrinking, so he thought he needed to get some more qualifications to access a different career. He began think about a teaching career. Colin Ross was a lecturer in the Art Department of what was then Newcastle Polytechnic, now Northumbria University, and encouraged Johnny to enrol. So, he set out on teacher training course in 1965, qualifying in 1967. Many folk musicians opted for teaching in the early sixties, as the job allowed them to do lots of gigs all over the country, but not Johnny. "The desire to live the semi-self-sufficient life, and reading John Seymour's book, plus a childhood reminiscence of all things rural, led me to the idea that teachers' holidays may not be for more bookings, fame, and self-esteem, but a chance to grow veg, brew beer, keep bees, and worry about broody hens, ducks, guinea fowl and geese. If ye can

The Bridge

try it, dee it, even if ye mek a mess on it!!!" [John Seymour was an early pioneer of self-sufficiency. The book he mentions was maybe the 1963 book *On my own terms*, which definitely sounds like Johnny Handle.]

The Bridge

Johnny feels that the time at the Liberal Club had "lent dignity to the thing", but like many others at that time felt that this revival was going to be a significant movement, with excitement in the air as large numbers of people were attracted to the clubs that had sprung up round the country. The move to the Bridge brought a very quick response from the punters. The club, of course, had a very high calibre of residents, arguably the best in the country, but few others had a Johnny Handle, who had already established a reputation as an entertainer with a wide range of talents. The upstairs room at the Bridge was perfect for what was to become one of the leading clubs in the British folk revival. A typical Thursday night would have three or four of the residents allotted to do most of the performing, with thirty minutes for "floor singers". The rest of the residents would be in attendance, but taking a back seat for the night. Despite having started their own club, the Elliotts were still coming.

Johnny had also been playing a melodeon of his own after borrowing one from Laurie Charlton, but it limited him in the keys he could play. The club residents reckoned such an excellent piano player would find the change to accordion an easy one, so they found one and presented it to him one night at the club. I never heard him play the melodeon, but he had found "It was easy to play because it's just like a mouth organ". No doubt he thought of the new instrument "a piano at right angles". He did pick up an amazing number of instruments very quickly.

Soon after the move to the Bridge, Ray Fisher married Colin Ross, and settled down to married life in Monkseaton. She was already an established singer from a legendary Scottish Glasgow family, her mother originating from the islands. Older brother Archie took her under his wing, doing gigs and featuring regularly on the STV programme *Hootenanny*. (It has always been the case that the Scottish media have supported folk music, whereas the English media seem to find it embarrassing. Archie ran the best such programme on Radio Scotland for several years, two hours on a Saturday night.) Johnny says of Ray "She came down and was a big fish in a little pond. She had style and presentation, and knew how to handle an audience. Her guitar style was used to great effect." Ray was a professional performer who delivered a mixture of traditional songs and ballads alongside more contemporary songs of great wit and salty humour with a relaxed, compelling manner. She maintained her status of "doyenne of Scots women singers" despite living the rest of her life on Tyneside. Alas, no longer with us, greatly missed.

In 1964, Johnny's second wife Alice had got the job of caretaker of the Black Gate, the original gatehouse of the castle, just over the road from the Bridge. The job included a flat, so naturally they moved in. (The downside was the 92 steps they had to climb up to it from the street!) What a windfall this turned out to be, a perfect place for parties, après-club sessions, and putting up guests. The Black Gate housed two important collections. The first was the library of the Antiquarians' Society, which provided Johnny with a fertile hunting ground for local materials. The second was a permanent display of Northumbrian pipes, and the Pipers' Society used to hold their meetings there. It must have been very tempting for him, and the

The Black Gate

Society had a practice set, so he borrowed these and "had a go. Not very hard, you just lift one finger off at a time. Well, what can you play on a gig? Chevy Chase?" Nobody can deny that Johnny lacked confidence, but pipes are somewhat different from other instruments. He used them on gigs, perhaps before he should have done, until Forster Charlton (by now one of two resident pipers at the club) got hold of him and said "You're doing it wrong. You've got to start again". So Johnny spent a whole fortnight just playing the drones. "Wait till the drones get automatic then you can concentrate on melody on the chanter." Forster and Colin were already making and repairing pipes, but "had trouble with reeds", Johnny's narrative being followed as usual by a lot of technical detail. Johnny had to have a go at this of course, and set up a "workshop" at the end of one of the galleries at the Black Gate. It must have been very cramped, but he managed to make a chanter, and turned half the drones on a tiny lathe. The professional pipe makers, of which there are now many, Colin Ross amongst the best, make most of their own parts, but working where he was, Johnny used fishing rod ferrules instead of turning brass. He has also learnt the "half longs", elbows-blown pipes from the Scottish borders with a chanter similar to the highland pipes. "I always had the lust, should have paid them more attention. If you got a Burns night or New Year gig, it was important."

Many of the instruments he has learnt have been given him by well-meaning people. These include an Anglo concertina, a "round-backed mandolin. Very difficult to play, the strings are too close together", and a zither. The last was courtesy of "a bloke who hung around the fringes of the club, enjoying the social life. We trusted him, and he came back to the parties. One day he vanished, upsetting his girlfriend greatly, and owing £10 to Paddy Foley". The club duly paid this, and Johnny was cursing this man on both counts, until returning to the Black Gate, he found a parcel containing a melodeon and a zither. So all was forgiven. A similar instrument, the autoharp, he got many of, especially from a binman in Gateshead who frequently found them on his round. At one time, he had three hanging on the wall. But he could certainly play it (not the most difficult instrument in the world though).

Johnny at Edinburgh Festival, 1962 (Brian Shuel)

Two important newcomers

Tom Gilfellon, a Stanley lad, who had been a resident at the oldest folk club in the country, Harry Boardman's Wayfarers club, was by 1964 an established singer and guitar player nationally. He had attended one of the early nights at the Jazz Club, when he first saw Louis and Johnny, both to become role models for his development as a folk singer. He went several times to the Barras Bridge, where at the tender age of 15, he was equally fascinated by the ladies in the bar as the music upstairs! He was already a great flat picker, modelling himself on Rambling Jack Elliott (later he developed an equal respect for the Birtley namesake). However, the young Tommy had a rock band in Stanley, which was out every night, and making money. On Thursdays, the folk club night, he had an A Level class, and so did not see much more of Johnny before he went to Manchester University. By 1962, he was firmly established at the Wayfarers' Club. (Tom and I were following parallel paths, he being from Newcastle but a student in Manchester, I being a Manchester lad and a student in Sheffield. So there were occasions when our paths crossed). Tom got both Johnny and Louis down to the Wayfarers' as guests on many occasions, where of course both were very popular. He reckons that it was seeing these two doing material from their own region that caused Harry to switch to doing Lancashire material. This, of course, meant him doing a lot of research, and the material he found was quite different, and nothing like as musical or exciting as the Geordie songs, of course. Tom, in his inimitable way, says "He invented the Lancashire tradition". I think there's more to be said about that, but before we move on, it is highly surprising that even with his ability and reputation, he had to go before the Bridge committee before being accepted as a resident. Laurie Charlton, then Chair of the committee "was a stickler for the rules". Tom, of course, added a new dimension to the club. Johnny's four-string guitar, with its banjo tuning, had been central to his repertoire, but of course with Tom joining in, this was no longer needed.

A story which illustrates the effect club residents were having elsewhere in the country is when Johnny and Tommy had a gig at the Watersons' club in Hull in 1962, then on the outskirts of town. Next day the two went walking around the docks. When Tom lit a tab on the petroleum dock, they were, let us put it politely, "ushered off". "So, seeking for further amusement" they finished up having beer and sandwiches at a pub called the Blue Bell. The wireless was playing *Woman's Hour* which by sheer chance featured Johnny and Alex Glasgow. The landlord comes in and says "I like that", so Tommy, pointing at Johnny, says "It's him". As a result, the Hull Folk Club transferred to the Blue Bell, forthwith, and for many years the two were synonymous. Points indeed!

Just before Tom returned from Manchester, a lad some years younger, in fact still at school, had started coming to the Bridge. He was Alistair Anderson, and at first came with his mate Dave Richardson, later of the Boys of the Lough. They had an interest particularly in dance and tunes, and he was knocked out by Colin's fiddle playing during the interval. But within a couple of weeks, the incomparable Scottish traveller Jeannie Robertson was the guest. Says Alistair "It was like she was from another planet. I'd never heard anything like it. She was riveting. But after singing, she was an ordinary, canny body". He was also very surprised to see another splendid Scots singer he'd seen on TV, and here she was, clearly one of the crowd. It was Ray Fisher of course, who by then was living on Tyneside with husband Colin. Ali was seeing the magic of folk music for the first time, and was drawn to it like a magnet. He was starting to pick out tunes on the mandolin, but one day he saw his first concertina. It had been his mate's grandfather's instrument, and was sitting in a display cabinet in his mate's front room in Wallsend. He borrowed it, and within a short time, he would accompany Dave Richardson singing songs from the recently published *The Singing Island*, and regularly get a spot at the Bridge. The rest, they say, is history, as he quickly established himself as the foremost concertina player in the country.

A couple of things need saying at this point. One was that the club closed for the summer, a fact which led to the formation of the Birtley Folk Club ("Why do they close? Let's start our own"). The other was the character of the landlord, Paddy Foley and his wife Norah. Paddy was a 25-stone ex-boxer, and you didn't mess with him. Tom remembers a night when with one hand on the bar, he leapt over it, hammer in hand, to sort out a bunch of trouble causers. But he loved the folk crowd, and would make contributions, such as the time when he brought to the club a famous Russian opera singer then appearing at the Theatre Royal. I don't know how long the turn lasted, but it went down a storm amongst people who were not interested in the genre. Laurie Charlton was the natural MC at the club, one which was in theory decided by "the committee", but after Laurie stopped coming, the job was effectively shared by Johnny and Ray. As to running the night, Johnny describes himself as "the fall guy". (Despite his reputation for behaving like "the cock of the midden", he can in private be very modest about his achievements.) The residents were complementary with their material. John Brennan was doing Irish songs, and rarely repeated himself, Ray Scots of course, and Laurie would do ballads, again mostly Scottish, but older songs than Ray. Tom Gilfellon was aware of his Irish background, but cautious of John Brennan whom he respected. He also had a lot of local songs, especially Tommy Armstrong ones, as both came from the Stanley area. He and Johnny effectively agreed to split the Tyneside stuff. Louis was doing mainly southern English songs, with an emphasis on maritime, but was increasingly absent from club nights, as he was by then cutting a dash nationally. He was "coming and going". I spent a year in London from 1963 to 64, and saw Louis frequently as a resident of the Troubadour. One night he brought with him four callow youths – the first time I'd heard the Watersons.

The House of God and The platform

Following on from the more formal arrangement at the Liberal club, the room at the Bridge had a raised platform, on which the designated residents would sit. On the non-guest nights, about half an hour was given to other singers, who were effectively vetted for quality. Small wonder then that many were loath to get up, as the assembled residents remained on stage, one often making acerbic comments. Many's the eminent guest who has commented on this. Jim Mageean, who started going to the Bridge in 1963 aged fifteen comments: "It wasn't very democratic. Only singers and musicians they knew well got a spot. It took me nearly ten years to be asked. In my opinion this is why spin-off clubs like Birtley, The Marsden and The Gosforth started up." However, on non-guest nights, Johnny, Tommy and often Louis would end the night with a 'shanty-bang', which had a seminal influence on the man who later became "Shanty Jim".

There is no doubt that the drive for quality that Johnny and Louis had was what gave the North East its early lead in the folk revival, and the club spawned several professional folk musicians. Johnny also makes the point that in the early days, volunteers from the floor would do the same song every week, which was boring, whereas the residents actively learnt new songs to sing at the club. The downside was that they got a reputation for eliteism and discouragement of other performers. When Johnny talks about the "dignity" of the club that started at the Liberal Club, he means that there was more of a concert presentation. However, it was the audience that started to shush up people who were chattering during songs. Compared with the more relaxed times at the Sink, and the other local clubs which were now springing up, he says that the Bridge had acquired the reputation as "The House of God". This was the situation in the first half of 1965, when a significant event took place well away from Tyneside, which we will look at in the next chapter.

The reaction of the committee was not to make concessions, but to keep Thursday night as it was, and start up another night, once a month on a Tuesday. This would be quite a different experience. As Thursday by now included tunes, pipe duets, and John Doonan, a ceilidh night was suggested. Colin had been playing for EFDSS dances, and although the Cheviot Ranters had been playing for barn dances in the Alnwick area for years, and were known nationally due to regular appearances on radio, they had not been seen on Tyneside. Nobody knew anything about dancing, so the Tuesday night would need a caller. Enter Graham Binless, the local EFDSS man who welcomed the idea of doing a more informal night, and who became central to these monthly nights. And the band! Colin, Johnny, Tom were soon joined by Forster and John Doonan. The Tuesday nights became popular very rapidly, and later there were ceilidh nights at the Birtley club, with a massive ad hoc band. Many of the people who came had no idea how to dance, but they quickly learnt, and found it enjoyable.

Eventually, the band on Tuesdays was anybody who turned up (who was brave enough), including the young Alistair Anderson, it being an ideal opportunity for him to develop the concertina, playing the dance music of Northumberland he was coming to love. He enthuses about Graham Binless, the caller, or "dancing master", who had a way of making things much more interesting to the young audience, than they would find at the somewhat refined EFDSS sessions. With a band driven by Johnny and Colin, it took off, starting with a few songs, a dance, a few songs, another dance, and so on, eventually becoming many dances with some songs. This would be 1965, and just as Folk Song and Ballad had been a major pioneer in the song revival, so the ceilidh nights were leading the field in the dance revival. This was demonstrated at Sidmouth Festival a couple of years later, when they ran a late-night extra which the High Level Ranters ran several nights because there were few others who could do it. (The group is considered in the next chapter.)

As people welcomed the informal atmosphere, they started to run these nights fortnightly, alternating as either a ceilidh or a singaround, which had been so successful at Birtley, and seemed more natural. People could have more conversation than the weekly Thursdays, whose residents took a back seat. And let's face it, the dance would allow more of a "boy meets girl experience". Graham and Johnny would be MCs for these nights, although other callers were encouraged. More performers from other clubs started coming, finding it good not to have to be so quiet. It was on these nights that they also started a new sword team, which included no less a person than Alistair Anderson. Johnny also suggested they had a Tuesday listening to records on the Dansette (for younger readers, this was one of two commercially available record players. Louis Killen had experienced this sort of "recital night" in his jazz days at the Roma Caffee). On other nights, they would have a speaker, such as Tony Foxworthy, the regional EFDSS man, to talk about English customs. Then he realised that if the Thursday club had a guest, they could do a talk on Tuesday and a gig at another club on the Wednesday (The Seven Stars at Ponteland, or the Birtley club. Bert Lloyd and Paddy Tunney did this). After the talk, there'd just be drinking and crack.

Like other folk clubs, people with a shared interest, especially one that was growing so fast, tended to do other things together. Johnny emphasizes how the Tuesday night led to many social groups. The "Club Hiking Group" was the most popular of these, meeting on Sundays. Then there were the bus trips to the Alnwick Gathering, weekends camping at Alwinton, and Saturday nights at the Bird at Elsdon. All these social occasions drew people from other clubs, friends of residents. Some people would come to the Black Gate bringing drink and sleeping bags.

Gaining experience as an entertainer

Johnny, as well as being central to what's just been described, was increasingly busy with solo folk club bookings, and was one of the few folkies who could do gigs at Working Mens' Clubs, still occasionally sat in with his old jazz mates, and could happily play the piano as background for some of the larger hotels in the area. Regarding social clubs, which most folkies have been unable to make any impact on, he showed no fear, musically or socially. He had extended this aspect, doing the social clubs with a "concert party" consisting of John Steele on drums (later of the Animals), and brother Brian on guitar, with Johnny on piano of course. They'd start with *Ain't misbehaving*, and *Dinah*, then The Everly Brothers and Duane Eddie. This was 1958, the year the folk club started, and Brian remembers they'd get between £2 and £4 a night. This would be just before Johnny's conversion to folk music, and Brian followed Johnny's lead being involved in several bands on Tyneside. The two brothers are occasionally seen playing "duelling piano", a highly entertaining novelty act which needs a lot of skill. But as Brian says, they never ever practised this stuff. One thing about Johnny that I've noticed over the years, when only a duff out of tune piano was available, he could make it sound passable. I, as a very limited player, was amazed how he could "play between the cracks". Brother Brian explains this by observing that instruments in social clubs were cheap and nasty, and Johnny learnt this lesson early on. The revelation only came to Brian ten years later with the John Doonan band. Quote "he has always been a busker, and I've followed him. It is his nature not to play the same thing twice". Maybe it's an aspect that carries on from his jazz days.

Speaking about the piano, of which he is the master, everybody I've talked to remembers his piano dismantling, which he did wherever there was one available. It started with one of the concert parties just described. "Well I got to this club, and something was wrong with the piano. So I up with the lid, and found some women's underwear. They had apparently been left by the magic man from the night before." He immediately spotted this as a great gimmick, so he pretended that there was a problem. In his standard act, he'd remove the front panels, quickly followed by the lid. Next, he started playing it deliberately out of tune à la Les Dawson, removing individual keys ("that's oot o tune"), throwing them to people in the audience. On later occasions, both audience and management were kind of expecting this, and knew he would put the instrument back together in working order. However, it did occasionally go wrong. Gary Hogg, singer and composer of comic verse, recalls an early night of the Cramlington Folk Club, where he had agreed with the pub landlord to have the piano restored, the cost of £80 to be shared (the club entry was at that time 20p!). There it was, on the night, all sparkling and fit. Johnny predictably started to take it apart, when the landlord looked in to see what was happening. Now, he was a big man, ex-army, and he was going spare. There was panic all round, but Gary managed to smooth things over. Johnny himself remembers doing Lincoln Folk Club, which had a brand new piano owned by the publican. Suffice it to say, as soon as he started on the act, the manager terminated the night, and ended the club. Back at the pad, everybody seemed happy. It turned out that they'd decided to change venue, didn't know when, but he had decided the matter! A similar story is told by Dave Normanton. Dave was calling for a band which included Johnny, which they'd had for several years. The venue had just bought a brand new piano, and had locked the instrument. Dave had to work very hard to persuade management to let him have the key, then he let Johnny know, and as Dave says "the switch was thrown". Not only did the piano get stripped, he started removing keys while still playing ("I don't use this one") and throwing them round the audience. The band never got the gig again.

Then there is the story of how, just after moving into the Black Gate, he learnt of a piano for sale in an auction in Gallowgate. He won the auction, and then had the job of taking it away. Well, finances being limited, he started singlehandedly wheeling the piano across town. Now I reckon this was about half a mile with some slopes, and many sets of traffic lights to negotiate. He says he saw several people he knew who commented, but did not help in any way! This should have been filmed. Today, many people would have videoed the event on their phones. After this epic trek, he then had the job of getting the thing up three floors of a tower built in the thirteenth century via a winding narrow staircase.

Different people in the North East have different stories about this, but I this is Johnny's. "Aa went ower the road to Paddy Foley's (The Bridge), and bowt a few pints for some of me folk friends who happened to be there. At closing time, aa told them about the piano! 'Nee bother' they said."

Then there was Basil Clough, Northumbrian piper, a draftsman, and somewhat eccentric. Johnny saw him as having something of a military bearing. Basil regularly ran nights at country pubs, taking people like Johnny along to entertain the locals. Jean, Basil's wife, had a classically trained voice, and played the harp. Basil would sing "Wor Nanny's a Mazor" with pipes and with only a trace of an accent. Elsdon was his favourite place for concert nights, with supper served at nearly midnight. Then there were the shepherd's and hunt supper nights, at Whittingham in the north of the county. These, he remembers, were set up with a strong hierarchical arrangement. The Duke and other landowners and worthies were on the top table, the farmers on the next, then a table for the shepherds, then hinds, then entertainers. There were elaborate toasts, replies, and smutty jokes, in between which an entertainer would be called upon. When Basil had taken Jean with her harp, they had all been much more restrained, so he was wont to take Johnny on guitar instead. He of course was no barrier to rural ribaldry. However, he got fixated with the harp, to the extent that when he visited the Leeds hotel when on Teesside, there was a huge picture of a harp hanging on the wall, actually a poster for Guinness. He asked the landlady could he borrow it? As he was a draftsman, he copied the harp at work, sent the drawing to Colin who made him a harp. Ironically, they demolished an old piano to provide the wood for the job. It worked quite well at the occasional hunt supper. (Years later, I got a gig for Tyne Tees Television where I had to dress as a minstrel and needed a harp as a prop to me singing Chevy Chase –Johnny of course still had the harp, so we were complete. I have to say that the incident does me no credit. Not only did I have to wear tights, a silly hat, and play the harp, it was decided that viewers would not be able to tolerate more than four verses of the ninety-two verse epic, but I missed Pete Seeger at City Hall doing the Bridge's 20th anniversary concert. Oh, the shame…..)

Quite early on, Johnny got TV and other work outside the folk club scene. First there was *Sunderland Oak*. Philip Donnellan was a BBC producer with an active interest in documentaries about social change. With an ultra-posh accent and background, he became a virtual Marxist due to his experiences with people in working class communities. In 1961 he made this film about the deteriorating shipbuilding industry in Sunderland, which had a century before had been one of the biggest shipbuilding towns in the world. Donnellan liked to set his films within an appropriate musical background, and asked Johnny to compose music and songs. It was a great artistic and social success, and people mention it often. I haven't mentioned his songwriting yet, which is the subject of a later chapter, but it had started in 1958 with *Farewell to the Monty* about a dying pit and by 1961 there were seven songs, nearly all about the pits. It shows what a great impression the man was making, that Donnellan chose him for the job.

The reason for Donnellan choosing Johnny was the result of his role in the radio ballad, *The Big Hewer*. In 1961, Ewan MacColl, Peggy Seeger and Charles Parker, a BBC radio producer, came up to Birtley to collect material. Through Louis, MacColl met Johnny, and he put him on to the Elliott family. So impressed were they with the Elliotts that virtually all the actuality from the North East in the programme comes from them. This story has been told elsewhere[1]. Clearly Charles Parker was impressed with Johnny, and passed his name on to his filmmaker friend Donnellan. MacColl too was impressed, after getting background information from Johnny while he was working on *The Big Hewer*. One time Johnny was telling them about the importance of the leek in Geordie culture in his inimical way. Their obvious fascination encouraged him to exaggerate. They passed it to the NCB News Unit, who decided to make a film on the subject, centering on Johnny. He had already made films for this outfit, but unfortunately "at that time I didn't know that much about leeks, but since I was playing at Bottom Club at Dudley, I knew a few champion leek growers in the area, and was able to help." (Dudley is close to Ashington, still regarded as the centre of leek culture, where the prizes are massive. Even in 1961 a winner could get £100, and later a brand new car was awarded).

A year later he participated in Centre 42, an artistic movement with a strong political drive led by playwright Arnold Wesker who had a new idea for spreading the best of culture beyond the elite. He had criticised

---

1   Pete Wood, *The Elliotts of Birtley*, Herron Books (2008) pp. 52-59

Johnny on cover of BMG magazine, 1966

the Labour movement for neglecting the arts. The 1960 Trades Unions Congress passed a resolution on agenda item 42 to conduct an enquiry into the arts. Wesker's initiative meant a large number of folk singers appearing in various parts of the country. They would have to create songs and music, and just go into pubs and other public places and perform their pieces. A number of people found it a daunting task to impose folksongs on people who mostly weren't interested. No problem for our man – by now nothing could phase him. He was already much more than an ex-jazzer folksinger. He had become an entertainer, and could melt the frostiest of hearts.

In 1964 he was approached by Charles Parker and Ewan MacColl, who after their Radio Ballads series had been asked to make a series of half-hour programmes entitled *From the cradle to the grave*, looking at all aspects of life. The idea was to use up and coming composers from the folk scene as field workers to collect "the actuality". Graeme Miles got death, Archie got childhood, Cyril Tawney got something else, and Johnny got ……pubs! He thought he'd died and gone to heaven. They would take the cumbersome recording gear, go into pubs and question people. Johnny was collaborating with a poet from Belfast called James Simmonds. They would visit each other and do the business, with Charles present initially, then they'd make regular reports. Johnny's song *The old pubs* came from this, and has been a big hit over the years. He remembers the sheer graft of the work, where instead of recording the songs separately, they had to do it "to the dot" on top of the actuality. Again, yet another difficult task he could tackle.

So, by this time Johnny was well established as a folk singer and musician, a comedian, a songwriter and academic with a separate career, and above all was a superb entertainer. But things were about to shift up a gear on the musical front.

Chapter 4 The Folk Revival at its height

"Everybody sang Johnny songs" Gary Hogg

BY 1965, THERE WERE FOLK CLUBS IN EVERY MAJOR TOWN IN BRITAIN, AND several in every main city. A number of singers had become professional and were issuing LPs at regular intervals. Johnny and the Bridge Folk Club were well in the vanguard of this, with residents equal to or better than any in the land. At this time, very few people were playing music in these clubs, but The Bridge (as I shall call the club from now on) was exceptional in this regard, as we have seen. However, these people (Colin Ross, Forster Charlton, Tommy, and Johnny), though they might play some things as duos, were not yet playing as a band. But what is more important, they had caught the eye of the "folk establishment".

The birth of the Ranters

At that time, there were no folk festivals, which seems hard to imagine now. The only exception was Sidmouth, which had been running as a dance festival since 1955. It was in 1962 that this spread to song, so that by 1965 this aspect was expanding rapidly, reflecting the burgeoning folk revival. But in 1965, the EFDSS in the form of Peter Kennedy, decided to run a major folk festival devoted to song and music. The venue was Keele University just west of the Potteries. This event turned out to be a seminal event in the folk revival, with a distinct emphasis on source singers from all over the British Isles. Amongst other names, there was Jeannie Robertson and Jimmy MacBeath from Scotland, Packie Byrne and the McPeakes from Northern Ireland, and Fred Jordan, Scan Tester, and Bob Roberts from England. It was about this time that we began to talk about "revival singers", who were young, did not necessarily have a family background in folk songs, but had been drawn to them either from listening to the source singers or from going to folk clubs up and

Johnny, Colin, and Nan Fleming Williams at Keele, 1966

down the country. Anne Briggs, Martin Carthy, and Louis Killen were in this category, and were included in the lineup. Five hundred people were there that weekend, and hugely enjoyed what they heard. Notice that all the people mentioned so far, except for the McPeakes, have been solo singers. But Bob Davenport brought the Rakes with him, and Johnny and Colin were both there, mainly as separate musicians who performed in concerts as well as delivering workshops. But it was the impromptu events that Johnny recalls fondly, such as meeting with Bob Cann, the Devon melodeon player, as soon as he walked in, the two immediately having a tune session. On another occasion, there was an after-hours session run by Eric Winter, who was putting on his London mates and ignoring splendid guests such as Jeannie Robertson. People were already starting to leave, so Johnny left and struck up a session with Dave Swarbrick, Colin, and Nan Fleming Williams. Eventually, the hall emptied, and people were sitting on the stairs, mainly singers, listening to the music. "One of most amazing sessions I've ever played in".

The following year, Keele was repeated, and this time Johnny and Colin brought Forster and Tom with them. This was definitely a band, so they needed a name, and it did not take Johnny long to find one. Around the Alnwick area were one of the most famous bands in the area, The Cheviot Ranters, whose name derived from the rant, very much a Northumbrian dance. There they were, these younger men,

Early picture of the Ranters

playing Northumbrian tunes and songs, running a club just next to the High Level Bridge. What better than the High Level Ranters?

Later that year Topic Records issued an LP, *Tommy Armstrong of Tyneside*, a tribute to the "pitman poet" from Tantobie near to Tommy's home town, Stanley. This was an important album which helped to establish the North East as a vibrant place in the developing folk revival. It featured Louis and local singer Maureen Craik, and though it did not use the name, was a significant forerunner of the Ranters, in the shape of Johnny, Colin, and Tom. At the time, a lot of people criticised the use of piano on this album, and yet Johnny was absolutely right to use it. Armstrong was at his height in the Edwardian period and World War 1, when every pub and public place had a piano, as did many working class households. Jim Mageean comments: "I already knew several Geordie songs as I had been singing them in family parties from about seven years old. What Johnny introduced me to was the great wealth of such material there was around, particularly at that time the songs of Tommy Armstrong which he and Tommy Gilfellon often performed. I bought the Tommy Armstrong LP as soon as they released it and it was a huge influence on me". The band was evolving in a seemingly casual way, but was very active. Johnny's diary for the year 1966 reveals no less than 84 bookings for Johnny, mainly at folk clubs all over the country, with local workshops, and 21 Ranters' gigs, mainly local ceilidhs with some concerts. Although Johnny's diary used the Ranters' name, it does not appear that the various band members were aware of this. The lineup for these depended on availability, with a core of Johnny Colin and Forster, plus John Doonan and Tom on occasions, the caller being normally Graham. At the second Keele in 1966, the band was the three core, plus Tommy and John Doonan. John was very active as a musician in the Irish community of Felling where he was a shipyard welder, with his own band, a trio with him, fiddle and accordion. One St Patrick's day instead of going to work, they went to play in the Catholic club. Unfortunately, the TV people came along and they were filmed. I'm not sure that John himself appeared in the film, but once his mate's wife had seen it on the TV, they were rumbled. The wives stopped the other two from going out, leaving John bandless. According to Johnny, this is the reason for his occasional presence in the Ranters and the club during 65 and 66. (John Doonan never let on, the story comes from

Kevin or Michael, his two sons). Eventually, the trio band got together again, and he returned to his roots.

Interestingly, Alistair was not at the first two Keele festivals, though he was at a later one, probably 1967. Also, although he was playing various gigs with them, he was not aware of the band name during 66 and 67. He recalls playing a ceilidh at Bath for Tubby Reynolds, then organiser of Sidmouth Festival (not a lot of bands could provide this). Also, he did the Singers' club in London, all five of them in Colin's A35 van. In those days, to do a Saturday gig in London meant travelling overnight Friday to avoid all the bottlenecks on the A1, several towns like Darlington not having yet had a by-pass. It is difficult to pin down a definite sequence of events in this period. It is clear that different people have different memories, hardly surprising after fifty years, and with so much going on then. So Alistair remembers gigs not recorded in Johnny's diary, especially his solo gigs, when Johnny, who has always encouraged other musicians, would invite him along to play. What a way for a young man to gain experience! Tom, agreeing with me that during the period from mid-1965 to the end of 1967, the lineup was "a bit of a mobile feast", says "No one ever said 'This is the Ranters.' It was never defined, it just was." Regarding the first LP, he says: "John Doonan had gone, Alistair had arrived". In less than three years, the young man had put in enough effort to become a permanent member of what was to be one of the most important bands of the early part of the revival. Tom describes him as "One of the great workers of the world. Amazing, perpetual motion." Regarding the evolution of the Ranters, Ali remembers a definite move to reduce the size of the Tuesday night ceilidh band in order to do more songs, which they'd do on Thursday nights, with four or five people, leaving the Tuesday band still whoever turned up. This was undoubtedly the forerunner of the Ranters. How important were these developments to the by now seventeen-year-old Alistair? Did it take over his life? "Well", he replied "That's why I went to Ponteland Training College, rather than go to Uni elsewhere. I didn't want to miss out on what was going on in Newcastle." This was 1966, and he spent the early years of the Ranters as a student, qualifying in 1969, by which time the band had really taken off.

It is likely that Sidmouth Folk Festival saw the crystallisation of the group. In 1967, Johnny, Colin and Ray went down (for accommodation

The four in sombre mood

only, which was the norm at the time.) They clearly made a great impact, since very quickly after their return to Newcastle, they had a letter from Bill Rutter, festival director, inviting them back in 1968. This time he wanted the full High Level Ranters, which as well as Johnny and Colin, would also include Forster, Tom, and Alistair. Significantly, the group offered various talks, workshops, and street busking sessions, and were listed in the programme as a band. Ray, of course, was listed under "singers". Part of their success in later years was their willingness and clear ability to offer such a wide range of activities.

The first Ranters' LP was done at the request of Bert Lloyd, co-founder of the British folk revival, and then Artistic Director of Topic Records, easily the most important producer of albums throughout the early revival. He had felt the need to include Northumbrian music in the repertoire, and so prescribed the theme. The title was *Northumberland Forever*, and it was recorded in January 1968 by Bill Leader at Forster's house. The record was a big success, and although recorded in stereo, was issued in mono, to cut costs. But the group sound was vibrant, exciting to listen to, and steeped in their local culture, exactly right for the time. This was different from Cecil Sharp and the "Deep South", but also different from the Scots and Irish material which people had been weaned on. The record sold well, and gigs started coming thick and fast, with Cambridge, Cleethorpes, and Sidmouth festivals included later in 1968, with the by now established lineup of five. Forster, several years older than Johnny and Colin, after attempting the touring that came with success, eventually confided to the group at York railway station after one trip "This touring's not for me". And so, shortly after the first record, the group became the "fab four" of the next epoch.

Meanwhile, let's get back to Johnny himself. He was clearly becoming very popular on the folk scene. The year 1965 had marked a major change in his day job. At that time, he was still working in the coal industry at Newbiggin and Ellington collieries. As in 1962, when he took the job at Billingham, he was unhappy about the future of the pits, and must have been thinking too about the demands of a "proper job" limiting how many folk gigs he could do. So, with Colin's support, he enrolled on a two-year teacher training course at what then was called Newcastle Polytechnic, now Northumbria University. Being on such a course would allow him more time to do gigs, but after he qualified in 1967, a teaching job would allow him more latitude than he would have had with a job down the pit, as he was on full-time call out as a mine surveyor. So, not only would he have more freedom to do solo gigs, but the Ranters were ideally placed to do the up and coming new folk festivals, notably Whitby, Cleethorpes, Sidmouth, and Towersey, which ran during July and August, exactly when they were all available, and of course to expand the vegetable and poultry activities. (By then, the members of the Ranters were all teachers of one kind or another.)

Two more great club residents

Two other people became residents in this period, Benny Graham, and Christine Hendry. Benny is widely recognised as one of the finest revival singers in the country. He first saw Johnny aged fifteen at Shotley Bridge Folk Club, but a year later, in 1967, he had a motorbike, was able to get to the Bridge in Newcastle easily, and got to know him. He remembers the platform of course, on to which he was soon invited, and was pressured into learning new songs by Johnny and Louis -"learn this, learn that"- which ties in with the policy followed by these two in particular. One night Bert Lloyd was the guest. Says Benny

"It was awe-inspiring. No way I'm sitting behind him". So, he was a resident in the late sixties, before pursuing his theatrical career in the seventies. I asked him about Johnny being the "gaffer". "Well, he was always the gobby one, but he was always the master at filling the gap. He always lifted the night." So, he might have practised something new to sing on the night, but would often judge that something light-hearted was needed, and he would make the sacrifice.

Importantly for our story, Benny was starting to get gigs, so he got a van which was handy for a kip, and when Johnny broke his leg, Benny would drive him to gigs and of course Johnny had a stuffed parrot on his shoulder! He remembers particularly the drive to Kiveton Park, with Johnny in the back on crutches, a nightmare trip. Anyway, Benny became homeless about that time, and stayed with Johnny at Winlaton Mill for eighteen months, a testament to Johnny's generosity to his mates (He and Christine put me up when I was going through a difficult divorce in the 1990s). What impressed Benny was that he had more energy than three men. Irrepressible. He'd have had a drink at the club, or do a gig, but was still up at six next morning, letting hens out, or feeding the ducks, and then teach all day.

Chris Hendry first went to the St Andrews club run by Pete Shepheard and Jimmy Hutchison when still at school around 1963-64. There she heard the best of Scottish singers such as Jeannie Robertson and Norman Kennedy. She first sang there in 1964 aged 16, and soon became a resident. As a result of a club visit to the Marsden club in 1965 she got to know Ray and Colin and visited the Bridge for the first time. She describes the experience as fantastic, different from St Andrews, mainly due to the music, which gave it life and lift. A year later she started a Psychology degree at Edinburgh, but the music was now "getting in the way" as she went to the Bridge as often as possible. Perhaps the music was only part of the reason she started a teacher training course in Newcastle in 1967, but it was inevitable that she would soon become a resident at the Bridge. The presence of two "big hitter" Scots women singers might have been seen as a shade unnecessary, but Chris and Ray had different repertoires, so it worked a treat. The Bridge remained "fantastic", with the audience interest and enthusiasm willing her to learn new songs. Chris remembers Johnny in those days: "If he wasn't at the club it was different. Less life, despite the quality of the residents. He was definitely special, with a magical quality, who could relate to everybody, picking out people from the audience. Sometimes he went too far with this, but it was never done with malice." She didn't realise then how much he knew about the history of songs and music, because he tended to sing "throwaway" songs. "Yes, it was partly due to keeping the night up, but also because he felt that he couldn't tackle difficult songs, i.e. he felt he could not do the songs justice." We will return to this aspect in the final chapter. Chris remained in Newcastle until 1974, when she moved to Oxford then Bristol. But the best thing about this is that she moved back, in 1988. and married Johnny in 1994.

Other local clubs in the late sixties

Although the Bridge was the first folk club in the North East, the area quickly acquired many more clubs, as the folk revival gathered pace in the 1960s. This led naturally to a proliferation of groups, performers, and bands. Thus when Johnny's brother Brian Pandrich returned after three years in Canada, he took up the fiddle, and was encouraged to play with Jimmy Irvine, at the hugely popular South Shields club at the Marsden Inn, the resident band being the highly regarded Marsden Rattlers, led by Jim Bainbridge. Brian is a bit modest about those days (or forgetful), but Jim and Trevor Sheridan assure me that he was definitely occasional with the Rattlers, another moveable feast. Trevor says that Johnny was very helpful to the Marsden Club when they first started, with him and Colin and Ray often turning up on Sundays and passed on gigs to the band if the Ranters couldn't make them. The Rattlers became Jim Irvine's Harvesters, which included Brian on piano and fiddle. Later, Brian played with the John Doonan band.

As a result of his involvement with the Killingworth Sword Dancers, Brian helped set up the famed Tyneside band Stanley Accrington and the Third Division North with Dennis Ambler. Originally a ceilidh band, this outfit increasingly entertained, featuring the irrepressible band caller Dave Normanton. Brian has diaries where he was out playing seven nights a week. Whereas the Rattlers and the Ranters would do "in betweenies", Dave would entertain on the floor while the punters were having their pie and peas supper. Over the years, the band would include other Tyneside legends such as Ray Laidlaw and Phil Murray, who were later involved with Lindisfarne, Jack the Lad, Hedgehog Pie, the Doonan Family band and others. Though less traditional than the Ranters, these groups were a very vigorous part of the Tyneside culture, extending it to a much wider audience.

Brian was involved in running a folk club, the New Darnell club.. Touring guests would sometimes do both this club and the Bridge, and Martin Carthy once had this arranged. Unfortunately, he fell ill on the day of the Bridge, and the club got Vin Garbutt as stand-in. Vin was already well established nationally by then, but still, the MC felt it necessary to apologise for the guest doing his own songs. This of course was exactly what Vin was known for, but many folk clubs in the sixties operated such a policy, allowing only traditional songs to be sung. Interesting that nobody objected to Johnny singing so many of his own songs, which may reflect the nature of his compositions. We have already clocked Eric Burdon's acknowledgment of Johnny, but while we are mentioning later celebrities, Brian mentions Mark Knopfler as being seen at the Bridge, a Tyneside rock icon who has in recent years shown himself to be a closet folkie. Brian Pandrich was sharing a Jesmond flat with Sting's mate Gerry at the time, which is described vividly in the rock singer's autobiography *Broken Music* in which he mentions Brian's brother as "local folk legend Johnny Handle". Perhaps Tyneside rockers have been more influenced by the local music than other places?

On his return from Teesside late in 1962, Johnny himself had started a monthly folk evening at the North Seaton Hotel (Locally called the White Elephant) which attracted some of the locals who later became residents at The Cellar, Ashington's very successful weekly folk club, run by Doug Cadwell. Chris and Ken Self ran the club very successfully for many years.

Despite being so busy with the gigs, and by now having a teaching post in Hebburn, Johnny realised a long-held dream of living the country life. He moved to a house at Winlaton Mill on the outskirts of Gateshead, which had a half acre of mature garden attached to it. How he found the time is beyond me, but he soon had the veg growing, and kept various kinds of livestock ("I must away and bar in the geese and the banties" is a phrase I have often heard from his lips).

A golden era

The High Level Ranters ran from 1968 with the first album, to 1979, when Tom and Alistair left the group. Thirteen years of intense activity and development in several senses. Johnny reckons in the early seventies he was making more money out of music than he was out of teaching. What with the Thursdays, the ceilidh nights, the Sunday hikes, and all manner of socialising, Tom reckons that the Ranters took over his life. Alistair remembers all the sheer graft in the early days to research Northumbrian material. He and Dave Richardson actually hand copied the only copy of the *Northumbrian Minstrelsy* available, in the Newcastle City Library. (That was just before 1965, when the reprint was published in America. So often the case!). Colin too was providing items for the first two LPs

I asked Johnny what were the best clubs and festivals of the late sixties and seventies. He instantly said Sidmouth (Ranters), Bromyard (solo), and Towersey (Ranters). Cleethorpes Festival he described as "The beginning of the session movement". I couldn't help but agree. I was at the first Cleethorpes festival in 1968, and there were seven separate sessions going on in the pier bar. An altogether unforgettable weekend for many reasons. What Johnny remembers is that some of the guests, i.e. The Fureys, Dave Swarbrick, and The Ranters, needed money and could not get a sub from the festival. So they busked on the beach, and the money rolled in. Imagine these people doing that now. Anyway, they spent it at the bar. He rolls off the names of clubs he could ring in those days, and get a gig as a minimum, usually a tour. Herga in London, Swindon, The Nova Scotia in Bristol, Dicky Bond at Malvern, Ken Penny at Exeter, The Yetties, Cheltenham with the Songwainers. There was a circuit round Birmingham, that not everybody got booked at, but you stayed with a Catholic family which meant you had to go to mass on Sunday morning. Then you would go to lunch at the pub and have a session. The Campbells would book him at their Birmingham club, then there was Shrewsbury, Newcastle-under-Lyne, and Stoke. There were two clubs at Chester, Friday and Sunday. These came up "regularly as clockwork." And then there was always the Grove at Leeds. Mostly the Ranters would do festivals, but some clubs would book them. As ceilidhs grew more popular, the Ranters would get gigs with a club and a ceilidh. Bradford Topic, one of the earliest folk clubs in the country,

The first Ranters' LP

and still going, were the first to do this. Hull was always important, and he started going down there before the club moved to the Blue Bell. (We had a good story in Chapter 3 about this). Then the Grimsby folk came over, which led to gigs there, then Boston, which he did regularly, followed by Lincoln, where the landlord dropped the lid on the piano as he was playing in order to get them out of the pub. Johnny said he'd waive the fee (well, to be fair, he had started dismantling the piano by then) but the club organisers laughed and said they were planning to move the next week anyway because nobody could stand the landlord.

As mentioned, some of the larger clubs began running ceilidhs on a separate night from the club, or mounting a special day like Haddenham, when the Ranters could shine in many departments, concerts, dance, and workshops. Often it was difficult to fit in the demand for band and solo gigs, and the latter definitely decreased during this period, whereas Alistair's naturally increased. And Johnny made no solo albums during this period. As early as 1971, his diary lists 111 solo gigs, and sixty Ranters' gigs, a gig every other day. Regarding the workshops, the group had oodles of topics to offer, the widest range by Johnny of course, which was not the case with every group. I remember the first or second Cleethorpes when Finbar Furey, a Uillean piper of few words but lots of action, being programmed on the Sunday morning for a workshop. He sat on the stage, looking completely at a loss, played a set of jigs, followed by silence. Eventually, he said "People often say to me, 'Tell me Finbar, why do you play so fast?'". A brief silence, then he said: "I can". I don't remember much of the rest.

Other things Johnny recalls were just for fun. Potto is a village in North Yorkshire where the Tynesiders, the Hull gang, and people from Teesside would have camping weekends at a farm in the hills, with dances in the barn, and much "daft carry-on". The North East folkies were just getting to know each other. Now they'd call it "bonding". Or a ceilidh at the "Poly", now Northumbria University, during Freshers' Week, with 400 students. The band was still doing this very lucrative gig when I was with them in the early eighties. What I remember is, amazingly, the women on one side of the room, the men on the other. Did the sixties never happen? We had to force them into meeting each other. Of course, the youngsters were then not interested in folk, and had come from all over the country, and were new to each other. I think that's me in charitable mode.

The City Hall concerts

When the Ranters became established nationally in the late sixties through their records and the rapidly developing festival scene, where they were in their element, the pressure was on them to go full time, as a lot of people were doing. The Spinners suggested this to the Ranters, so just as with the Liverpool group, the Ranters tested the waters by mounting a series of concerts at the City Hall in Newcastle. At the time, this was the biggest concert hall in the town, with a capacity of just under 2000. The first concert, in 1970, sold 1600 tickets, with two later ones attracting about 1200. Quite astounding for a local folk group. A review from the first concert is quoted with relish by Alistair: "Nor did they paint in borrowed colours", a reference to the fact that most of their material was local. Who else could do these kind of concerts? There were spots on the TV, causing people to come down from the northern areas of Northumberland they rarely stirred from. Billy Pigg, the Northumbrian piper, was mentioned on the TV and at the concert. The Northumbrians whispered "Do you mean our Billy?" They found it difficult to believe that a musician in their area could be mentioned in these circles. Billy hardly got out, preferring to play at home, whereas the slightly younger piper Joe Hutton observed this, and would later turn out for many events, provided that they did not coincide with his work as a shepherd in the foothills of Cheviot. The folk revival, as Ali suggests, was having some effect on the tradition.

By this time, the band was in full swing, with as many gigs as they could take. Ali remembers about 1970 they had ten gigs in a fortnight, the closest in Wooler, the furthest in Manchester, and all four of the group were full-time teachers. He thought that this was a bit unfair to the kids in his class, and was becoming increasingly concerned about the old Northumbrians not being recognised. "Billy's just died, and nobody's heard his stuff". As a result of these thoughts, Ali became professional in 1971. But he was to stick with the Ranters for another eight glorious years.

The first LP was a major success for Topic, but when it came to the second album, Bill Leader had set up his own label, and the group elected to go with him. At the time, Topic were seen as a tad old-fashioned. Not only that, Bill wanted to have more exciting covers, and to drop the price (Ali remembers in the early 70s staying with people in the States who had had shelves full of LPs, which was not the case in England. He compares a price of £1.30 with 10.5 p for a pint of beer memorably features in Johnny's song *Danny's* "ten and a half for a pint of scotch, why hinny man ye canna gan wrang".). The second LP, *The Lads of Northumbria,* released in 1969, had mostly local material, but reflected more their standard repertoire, including some Irish and Scottish tracks.

Johnny came into his own with the third LP, *Keep Your Feet Still Geordie Hinnie* in 1970. Entirely Geordie music hall, recorded by Bill

Leader at Balmbra's in Newcastle's Cloth Market (of *Blaydon Races* fame), then still existing as a small music hall, with a proscenium arch. Tommy and Johnny did the singing, aided and abetted by the other two Ranters of course, but .in order to get the sound of the old pit orchestras, he used his old jazz buddies, including Colin Beale, clarinet, Ronnie Mclean, trombone, and Tom Waugh, bass. As he says "It could not possibly get better than this. The LP was important because prior to that there'd only been straight albums by people like Owen Brannigan. The band was big, and difficult to record, so it has some rough edges, but is surprisingly good in spite of this"

The American and Australian tours

The same year, the Ranters had their first American tour. This centred around a weekend festival at Penn State University, for which they were offered a fee of a thousand dollars, payable on completion. Additional funds were found from concerts in Northumberland which promoted a newly formed rural arts initiative. After the festival was over, the lady chair of the liaison committee put on a cocktail party, where the cheque would be given. A very swish do, with lots of University high-ups, and what with the long speeches, canapes, and cocktails, the four got somewhat brassed off. However, they had got very pally with the students, who'd been to the concert and the dance, and who had a party, with beer waiting for them. So, quite quickly they arrived at the party in a log cabin, having a good time, and it being February, there was a lot of snow outside. A snowball fight was agreed, with a USA team versus the rest (Ranters, Canadians, and some Europeans). The rest would defend the house, and the USA would attack, and it started with a "rebel yell". Says Johnny "Well, these Americans employed guerrilla tactics by picking us up and throwing us into snowdrifts. Not very sporting. Honour was satisfied, and we sat steaming around the log fire when I realised that the cheque had fallen out of my pocket. The other three had disappeared and gone off on various billets to sleep." So he organised a search party.in the dark, with torches, which of course failed to find said cheque. At breakfast they had to tell the lads the bad news. They definitely were not amused, told him to go and grovel to the woman, and said "We think it's time you stopped handling the money." (This story came from Johnny in answer to my question "Were you in charge of the operation?")

Another major trip abroad was the Australian tour of 1976. I heard this story either from Tom Gilfellon or the Ozzie lads who ran the second tour in 1981. They'd arrived in Melbourne after a 27-hour flight, went straight to a performance at the National Festival then played at a party all night without any sleep. The Australians were utterly knocked out by the quality and the stamina of these four poms. I have always thought that it was on the strength of this that they had the group back for a second tour. Anyway, Johnny thinks enhancement has been at work in the telling of the tale. What I didn't know till now was that they'd set up a tour with an agent who had welched on the deal at last minute, and informed them by telegram. The only gig was the National Festival at Melbourne, which was then low key, hardly enough to pay for the air fares. However, they'd paid deposits and got visas etc., so decided to go if only to get the money from the agent legally. They were looking at two weeks in Oz with no other gigs. Johnny does remember some kind of party, where he climbed on the table, so they obviously put on a bit of a show and impressed the other guys. And no waving of the fiddle bow from Colin, "now then John…" He also remembers performing in O'Connor's pub, with foaming jugs of beer. "It was just a good night, they were going strong as well. Matiness. Goodwill. When we saw them at breakfast they said 'we're not having this'". So they got them enough gigs over the fortnight to pay for the flights, internal travel, and pocket money.

More Ranters' Albums

Meanwhile, the group had continued to make albums throughout the seventies. After the music hall LP had come *High Level,* with songs from all over and tunes mainly from the North East, and *A Mile to ride*, with mostly Northumbrian songs and tunes. The next, issued in 1975, was *Bonnie Pit Laddie,* Johnny's idea. A Single LP was not big enough for the subject, it would need to be a double, which Topic were not happy with. So to sell the idea to them, he extended the concept to areas outside the North East in the form of Scotland (Dick Gaughan) and Lancashire (Harry Boardman). Bert Lloyd was still influential at Topic, and on the back of the second edition of his book *Come all ye bold miners,* he supported the project. (The irony of this is that Bert's book was flooded with songs from the North East, though Dick and

The cover of "Four in a bar"

Harry were not short of material, and made fine contributions). *Rantin'
Lads* (1976) was entirely North East based, and the last Ranters' album
with the old group was *Four in a bar*, entirely devoted to North East
dance music, which reflected Colin and Alistair's deep and continuing
involvement with the music. The cover of the LP, issued in 1979, with
the four in the front bar of the Bridge with the stained glass window
behind, has become an icon of the group, Newcastle, and the seventies.

In sum, the eight albums issued by the Ranters in those eleven years
included fifty-three North East songs, and eighty northeast tunes. A
prodigious feat, and all of the highest quality. There is no other English
region, and no other band, which could have achieved anything like
that. But there was something special about this group of four, centering

on Colin and Johnny's unique sound, a remarkable musical pairing between two men of utterly different character and temperament. The other two were simply the best at what they did. As Tom puts it: "Me and Alistair were the technicians. The whole thing was symbiotic. The whole was greater than the parts."

There were of course many other folk groups around at that time. The earliest English ones were the Spinners in Liverpool, the Ian Campbell Group in Birmingham, and the Yetties in Dorset, all of which had started in the late fifties, and had become fully professional by the time the Ranters formed. In Ireland, the Chieftains and the Dubliners both started in 1962, and really took off internationally. The Scots groups such as Battlefield Band and Boys of the Lough, and the so-called "folk rock" groups like Fairport Convention and Steeleye Span started about the same time as the Ranters. The Ranters were unique in having day jobs, but still achieved great popularity especially on the burgeoning festival scene, and were regarded as the equal of most of the professional groups. As we have seen, the emphasis was on North East material, which they made as popular as the phenomenal growth of Irish and Scottish music.

Before we move on in time, I should mention two other aspects of Johnny's career. Starting in the late sixties, the local TV stations would call upon his services to illustrate a topic or news item. Thus the song *He's got them on the run* was written for a TV programme on Brendan Forster, the great local athlete. For a programme about the setting up of Beamish Museum, he'd do traditional songs. Tyne Tees set up a series of programmes on a range of topics, with an audience and a comedian, and Johnny would sing a song he'd made up. The only one he remembers is one about the army. The series was a flop, but it had a positive outcome. He was in the Musicians Union, but that was not enough – if you sang, you'd have to be in the Actors' Union, Equity. The producer did not want to lose him, so he was duly enrolled. The benefit was that this led to other lucrative gigs. On other occasions, a news item would come up, the production team would ring him (at work, one of several schools on Tyneside), and ask him for a song for the programme. Many's the time he would get on the bus into town, on the top deck, scribbling words and hoping he could put something together in time. One of these occasions, which led to the song *Penny for the Guy*, is detailed in Chapter 9. Another one, a recitation this time, *Little cottage in the country,* came about because he found media people somewhat pretentious and trendy.

Sometime in the late 70s there arose the "comic folkie", with a regional bias. So, led by Billy Connolly from the Glasgow shipyards, we had Mike Harding from Manchester, Max Boyce from the pits of South Wales, and Jasper Carrot from Birmingham. Faced with the success of these multi-talented people, who were comedians at heart, EMI saw other opportunites, based on the English regions. Johnny was clearly the one from the North East, most emphatically a Geordie, and not only a folkie, but a comedian to boot. He would most certainly do. Accordingly, they put up money for an LP, a live recording which didn't work out on Tyneside so was recorded in London which rather took the edge off it. It was called "A big lass and a bonnie lass", which was reflected by the cover which had Johnny with a girl who was bonny, but about twice his size. The project didn't work out, and EMI did not pursue it. I don't think Johnny had the discipline for a career controlled by the media, which has ensured he has stayed a local legend, to the great benefit of the folk revival and Tyneside's place within it. Incidentally, Tony Wilson (the Sheffield one) tells me that the cover of the LP won an online award as being amongst the top ten worst covers.

That he preferred this route is confirmed by the fact that he had not become a professional musician, which he might well have done several years earlier. He admits to being severely tempted, "as the diaries from 1969-1973 show, there were times when folk work exceeded salaries in teaching. I never believed in the patter that agents used to tell you about riches if you would travel about all over." Whilst he was mostly employed as a general teacher, he made significant contribution to music, either by being involved in taking the assembly, or volunteering a music syllabus where there was none. In the first case. colleagues being unable or unwilling to cope, "the lot fell to the music teacher. I examined the Hymn books, and worked on a more sensible repertoire with rather more swinging melodies or at least attractive accompaniments. As a practice was deemed necessary I took with me some support, while the teachers cowered in the staff room, clinging on to their coffee and woodbines." He loves talking in these disparaging terms, although as always, it's done mainly for comedic reasons. But he tackled the problem in typical ways, by offering the kids a singsong after going through the hymns. (*Oh you Beautiful Doll, My old man*). The kids of course rattled through the hymns so that they could have a longer singsong. But it was in class that he was at his best, going to all sorts of lengths to get them interested. So, he deployed coloured chord markers on chime bars, autoharp bars, and open tuned guitar necks, making it possible for a child or non-musical staff member to take a class. "Sounds mad but it works great, and once you've vidcocd them, they are very proud." In whistle making, justified as part of the craft syllabus, the fipple is made from electrical conduit plastic tubes and fit into the barrel tube which is made from overflow pipe for toilets and bathrooms. There was a skiffle project, which meant taking a troop of pupils up to Ringtons, the Newcastle tea merchants, where they took two tea chests back to school to make a double bass. "Junky guitars were a bit easier to get and we became adept at repairing them. Another craft job was to make a chord zither out of a wooden box, using old guitar strings, and buying in machine heads. A lot of these ideas were designed to get students with lower motor abilities to have maximum pleasure out of their music and song, although preparation and experiment took a good bit of my own time." These aspect arose from a conversation on how he learnt such a vast range of instruments, during which I found he was actually talking about his teaching experience. It became clear to me that not only was he an exceptional teacher, but he'd really enjoyed it.

Chapter 5 Pastures New

"Always the master at filling the gap" Benny Graham

THE RANTERS DURING THE SEVENTIES AS THE FOUR OUTSTANDING INDIVIDUALS Johnny, Colin, Alistair, and Tommy, and their glittering career in the seventies was described in the previous chapter. However, by about 1979, it was clear that Alistair's solo career had taken off to a degree that meant he couldn't sustain both. Not only that, as Ali says "Towards the end, the Ranters were having to turn down gigs and there were tensions between members of the band." The latter observation is shared by many people who knew them well. Mike Tickell asserted that the differences between the personalities created the seeds of their own destruction. Johnny comments that Ali was at that time getting a lot of solo work, but was good about not taking a gig if there was a Ranters' gig in the offing. There was a meeting at which they analysed the situation. "We were tempted, [to turn professional], but never wanted it. Tony Davis of the Spinners was being very encouraging, happy to set up contacts to help us". He then proceeds to tell an elaborate canal story as an analogy to say effectively that the Ranters "had gone too far. The outcome was inevitable. It wasn't acrimonious." Tensions between individuals he considers irrelevant. Tommy was increasingly playing with Chuck Fleming and Martin Matthews (which eventually led to the excellent, but short-lived Champion String Band). The upshot of this was that both Alistair and Tommy left the group at about the same time.

Despite the brilliance of both Alistair and Tommy at what they did, there is little doubt that the "engine" of the Ranters had been the musical chemistry that existed between Johnny and Colin. Such combinations rarely occur. So, in 1980 or thereabouts with the other two no longer there, what would they do? They were only in their forties, the sound was a successful one, so would they give up or continue with the band? I'd have given my eyeteeth to have eavesdropped on those conversations, but the decision was made to continue. How to replace the other two? Well, the group had always been the quintessence of Northumberland, and they'd need a musician to reflect the absence of Alistair. Jim Hall, a talented Northumbrian piper, fitted the bill, and Colin pushed for that, since he has always seen himself as more of a fiddler than a piper in performance despite his being a pipe maker of the highest calibre, and a central figure in the Northumbrian Pipers' Society. (I have to say that Colin playing slow airs on the pipes is hard to beat). So, Tommy was a singer – who would replace him? I think it should have been Benny Graham, a great mate of Johnny's, from Stanley just like Tommy, not a guitarist, but easily the best folk singer in North East then and now. He was utterly steeped in the culture. Maybe they needed all four to be instrumentalists. But they needed another singer. I was shocked to receive a call from Johnny inviting me to join the group. At the time, I was singing, with a good reputation, accompanied on guitar and concertina. I'd been playing tunes on the latter for some time, but was no more than competent. The same can be said for my guitar playing. I'd been OK with gigs on both, but I was no substitute as an instrumentalist for either Ali or Tommy. I didn't know Johnny very well at that date, but was surprised and honoured to be asked, so I said yes. In retrospect, I'm not sure it was the right decision for the group, but I did have some amazing experiences, and Johnny became a lifelong mate.

We set about making an LP titled "The new High Level Ranters" for Topic issued in 1982, which enjoyed only modest success I think. Soon after I joined, Johnny said to me. "We do ceilidhs, quite a lot actually, and Tommy played piano – so that's down to ye." Well, the piano was my first instrument, I'd got to Grade Two with Mr Axford, and then dumped it along with the School Choir and Sunday school aged thirteen or fourteen. So, I went for an extremely brief lesson from Tommy. "If it's in G, you do this" He played a descending series of chords as a vamp. "If it's in D, you do this". He played the same sequence in D. That was it. I was qualified to vamp with the Ranters on keyboard for ceilidhs. Jim Hall did the calling, so it was a 3-piece band. Colin and Johnny had been together for so long that although they had fixed sets for various dances, they used to amuse themselves by waiting until the very last minute before deciding what the next tune would be. It soon became a matter of seconds before one of them would spit the title out to the other, and if there was still time, i.e. the very last bar of the current tune, would hurl out the key over their shoulder to myself, some way away on piano. It was a complete waste of time doing that, because I have to tell you, gentle reader, that at the height of the night, with the noise of the band and the dancers, at that distance, and with a Geordie accent, "G","D", and "A" sound exactly the same. I very quickly learned to pick up the key of a tune, and so would be spot on by the second or third bar.

The highlight of my time with the band was undoubtedly the second Australian tour in July 1981. There isn't space for much of this, but here's a couple of stories involving Johnny. We had a van drive from Melbourne to Sydney, with a couple of gigs on the way. It was a fascinating drive for me, but Johnny had travelled the same route on the first tour, so he found things to do. He was very quiet, writing things in a little book, copiously. When we stopped, he gave me the book. It contained the chord sequences for every tune in the band's dance repertoire. What amazed me was that he hadn't needed an instrument to do this. Brain power, and real musical talent. But he had spotted my need, and had put the time to good use. He enjoyed everything in life, including food. One pad we had there was no breakfast at all, so on the second day, the day after the famous Botham test at Headingly, he went out, shouting at the cars about the cricket, and returned with bacon, eggs, sausage and mushrooms, and cooked it himself. The snag was that he got confused between pounds and kilograms, so they probably lived on the remains for the rest of the week. There was a kip in Sydney, an insalubrious place shall we say, where the breakfast was a pile of cheap sliced white bread toast, uniformly burnt, and sausages that had a liverish grey colour, the texture of rubber, and the taste only of sage. The hostess astonished us by producing these out of an electric kettle. The poet in him rose to the occasion: "And she gave to me boiled sausages, On the Parramatta Road"

Whilst enjoying my time with the band, I didn't feel it was working, mainly due to my not being a Geordie, so at some date between 1982 or 1983, I left. Then what would they do? Colin was having problems with his heart, and soon had the first of several bypass operations.

Jim Hall, though a great piper, had difficulties with busking, a band trait with the "fab four", Johnny didn't believe in practising too much, the trio would mean the dominance of music over song, and Johnny had three acres out at Bardon Mill which demanded much of his time. "The ties of the land. I'd had half an acre at Winlaton Mill, and I was trying to convert all that acreage into production. I wanted to be at least half self-sufficient, intended to be there for the rest of my life." I remember him planting apple trees there, which you don't do if you'll be flitting soon. Being out there also meant a lot of travelling involved, as well as bringing up a young family of four. At this time, the eighties and nineties, he was finding it difficult to get gigs and tours, because "It was satisfying to feed the needs of mother earth", a yearning that had started with his grandfather's place in Morpeth, and continued with the narrow strip beside the railway he'd had when living Holly Avenue in Jesmond. So, the three Ranters still left decided to continue, reverting to the original name, but doing far fewer gigs. Another Topic LP, *Border Spirit*, was issued in 1983, followed in 1990 by *Gateshead Revisited*, coinciding with the Gateshead Garden Festival, with a last LP *Bridging* in 2004. The three did their last gig in 2012, appropriately at a Forster Charlton memorial evening.

With the reduced programme of the Ranters, the eighties became a time for local ceilidh gigs, which needed one or two musicians and a caller. The second player was at first Geoff Hardisty, who was artistic director at the Queens Theatre in Hexham, and with Arts money flowing in, he was running a very popular folk events programme. To give readers a flavour of the sort of people who could confidently be booked in 1984, here is part of the programme for that year: Tony Capstick, Gordon Giltrap, Dave Swarbrick, Martin Carthy, Cape Breton Fiddlers, Cilla and Artie Tresize, Ralph McTell, Julie Felix, Kieron Halpin. Note that Carthy and Swarbrick were booked separately! Thirty years later, another local musician, Simon Haworth, is in charge at the Queen's, and running a similar folk-based programme. Here's the 2015 lineup: The Broonzies (Jez Lowe, Rod Clements, Maggie Holland, Chris Parkinson, Ian Thompson), Edwina Hayes, Benny Graham and Chuck Fleming, Steve Tilston, Eddie Walker and Frank Porter, Wildings, and The Andy May Trio. Well done Simon, for continuing a noble tradition, when folk clubs, even in the North East, are closing one by one.

The three in the eighties

Geoff, although a consummate musician, did not busk, so Johnny recorded all the sets for the dance and Geoff transcribed them, so he would have the dots in front of him at ceilidhs. Geoff played a very important role in the life of Johnny Handle of the eighties, as described later in this chapter. When Geoff wasn't available, Matt Seattle played fiddle, and when he wasn't free he'd use Chuck Fleming (never a shortage of first class musicians in the North East –Kevin Doonan and Stewart Hardy also featured!). With Chuck, Johnny saw other possibilities, and he asked me to join in a few ceilidhs prior to setting up the three of us as the Johnny Handle Band in the early nineties. We recorded one album, of Johnny's creations, at Geoff Heslop's studio in Elsdon.

The songs and tunes composed in this period reflect his rural lifestyle. Womens' Institutes, Fiddle and Accordion club, anything local. Fiddle and Accordion clubs are of course the backbone of the Scottish tradition, but Northumberland had and still has several clubs. A different culture from the folk scene of course. Well, Johnny once took me along to the Hexham Club, held at the CIU club in the middle of town. Once a year they would have a special night with a top Scottish band. Anyway, this year the Hexham Fiddle and Accordion Club booked fiddler Ian Powrie, who had become a legend in Scotland via the White Heather Club on the BBC, had emigrated to Australia, but had returned to become even more popular. He was supposed to do the gig solo, but brought a trio. This was an incredibly popular night, but Johnny managed to get us two tickets. There we were, two disreputable folkies in a crowded room, with the burghers of the town sitting in serried ranks with buttoned up overcoats in a respectful silence. We felt like two young schoolboys who had to be on their best behaviour. The warm-ups were the Northumbrian shepherds in the form of John Dagg, Will Atkinson, and Joe Hutton. A right contrast of cultures it turned out to be. When these three got up the conversation went like this: "Wae, what'll we play? Wae I divvent ken the furstun. Wae I divvent ken the second" They rambled on in similar vein before striking up. And they were excellent of course. Then it was Powrie's turn. Accordion, fiddle and drums. "One, two" and they were off, like clockwork. Different cultures!

The visit to Hexham CIU described in the last paragraph had brought up the importance of Jimmy Shand, a regular visitor to the Tyne Valley, and reminds me of when I first moved to the North East in 1974. I got to visit the Alwinton Border Shepherds Show, the last in the calendar in early October. It is a great setting, very near the Scottish border, with the hills behind the village clad in brown bracken, with traditional sports like hound trailing, terrier races, Cumberland wrestling, a Tug o' War, lots of tents selling stuff, the pipes being played in the beer tent, and drunk lads in an unofficial sport, shinning up the pole of the beer tent (a massive marquee, must be twenty feet high). In the evening, lots of people decamped to another favourite of Tynesiders, the Bird in Bush at Elsdon, for a massive singing and music session, I was knocked out by all this of course, but the thing that really stood out were the dodgems. Yes, they had a fair on the site as well. When the Wakes Week fair came to my home town in Lancashire in the fifties, the music they played through the tannoy were the hits of the day, Elvis Presley and Lonnie Donegan. What were they playing at Alwinton? Why Jimmy Shand, of course!

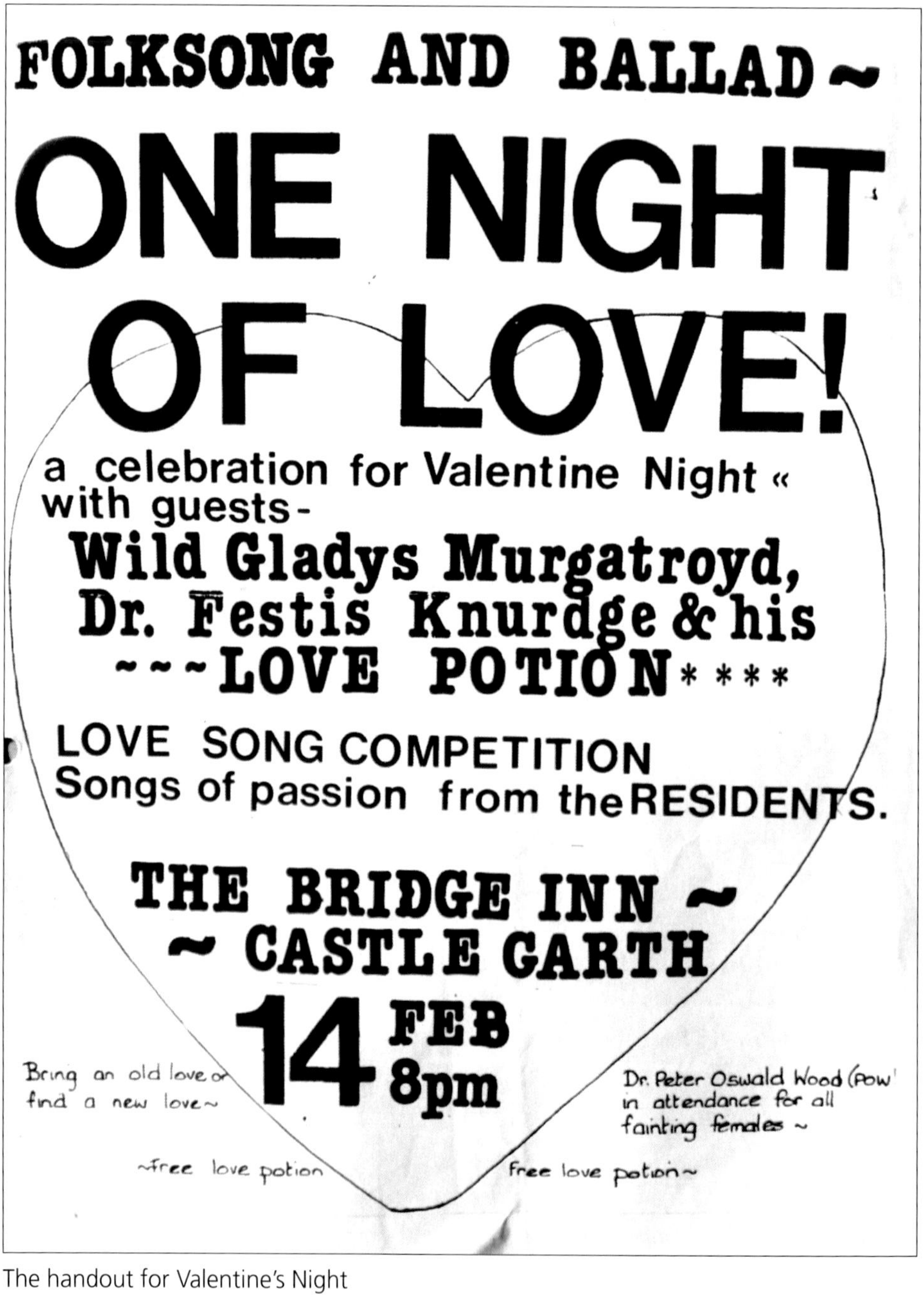

The handout for Valentine's Night

The shows

Johnny had been involved in "productions" quite early, starting with *Sunderland Oak* and *Centre 42* described in Chapter 3. Early on at the Bridge he'd scripted and had the residents perform jokey mummer's plays, and when he entered the teaching profession in 1965, had run several shows in schools, including nativity plays. At a summer school at the teachers' centre, he had volunteer kids working on Northumbrian and border ballads, where he would tell the story and they sang and read a few verses.

Before we turn to weightier productions, let us consider an occasion so typical of many in this man's life. It is sometime in the early nineties, the Bridge is still running, in the basement, probably still with Ray and Colin, Ron and John, and myself as residents. Johnny has become of "occasional visitor" class. Valentine's Day was a Thursday, so there was a special night. But nobody was expecting what happened next. Johnny appeared with two things, a script for a Valentine's night show, and a cooking pot full of ……..heart curry! The story of the script which he then enacted was based on *The Parted Lovers* where the "broken token", kept in a cardboard box, was, in fact, a pair of tights from a lass at Slaggyford, one leg was red the other blue. Her man's journey meant playing darts in the Bollockpool League (one of Mike Harding's inventions). Here they blunted Bold Jack's darts and gave him six-inch nails to play with. He was so successful at scoring double nineteen that they pressed him into service, sentencing him to "seeven lang yeears" in the Lancashire League. After this time, he comes back to Slaggyford. A rambling story involving lavish use of Lancashire and Scottish accents. He remembers this because he still has the script, but many spontaneous creations have gone unmarked, such as the Otterburn librarians' monologue described later in chapter 8. When reminded of such things, he says rather cryptically "I remember doing something. The Man with the drip on his nose". But he has the full script for *Double Nineteen* if you're interested!

Now let us look at some more important productions in Johnny's career.

Peter Cheeseman was a playwright and drama producer who pioneered theatre in the round at the Victoria Theatre in Stoke-on-Trent in the early sixties. He thought that productions should reflect the local community and involve the people, was of the Charles Parker school of political drama and like him, he used music as often as he could. Whilst many of his productions were to do with the pottery industry, the area also had coal mines, and many Geordies had migrated to the area as the inland pits of the North East had closed. Hence the connection with Johnny, who was commissioned to write and perform songs with at least two productions, *Miner Dig the Coal* in 1981, and *The Keelman's Hop* in 1984, which gave birth to his song *Lemington Keel* which he still often sings. The latter production featured the High Level Ranters, and I remember them wearing their keelman's rigs on Tyneside at that time.

About the same time, Johnny got involved with a Tyne Tees TV production of *Joe Lives,* originally a stage play written by Alex Glasgow featuring John Woodvine as the great nineteenth-century songwriter and entertainer Joe Wilson. The TV show featured Alun Armstrong as Joe, and Johnny contributed material, as well as accompanying his songs on piano and pedal organ. A "new journey" for Johnny, very different from his previous television experience. Geoff Hardisty was introduced earlier in this chapter, but he became very central in the eighties. "Not as important as Louis, but nearly. Without him, the brass would never have happened." What he means by "the brass" is two major productions initiated by him.

The Tyne Valley Suite 1984

The first, entitled *A Tyne Valley Suite*, was a lyrical look at the course of the North Tyne and South Tyne rivers from mountains to their meeting near Hexham, using song, music, and stories. It arose from Johnny's ceaseless search for new musical ideas, and Geoff's experience conducting some of the top brass bands. And he could score proper music, a skill rare in the folk world. So, Johnny wrote the script, and Geoff scored the suite for brass. They used the piper from the Ranters, Jim Hall, and fellow songwriter Terry Conway as another singer. Locally, there was the Haydon Bridge brass band and the Ovington silver band, so they planned to use them both. Unfortunately, a history of rivalry had ensured that these two bands were unable to work together, so the two were forced to put together a band from individual Musicians'

A view of the Tyne Valley

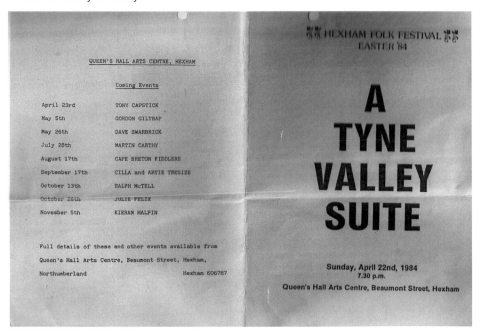

Part of the programme for Tyne Valley Suite

Union members in the area. Not only did Geoff have to re-score the music to accommodate these diverse people, a major event in the days before computers, but Johnny also felt the need to adjust his patter, which he now regards as somewhat gauche. However, I was there on the one night it was presented, at the Queen's Theatre in Hexham, and though I cannot recall detail, I enjoyed the night. Having just listened to a recording of the event, I am impressed by the brass, as I am with the rest. He has complete command of his subject. So, Terry does *The Ballad of Percy Reed* (has anybody ever done it better?) and his own immaculate compositions *Hawkhope Hill,* a hilarious account of Northumberland's re-housing of local people upon the construction of the Kielder Dam ("ye can have them half way up the bank, or else it's half way doon") and *Fare Thee Well Regality*, a passionate evocation of Hexhamshire, the region south of Hexham governed by the Archbishop of York in the middle ages. And Johnny himself, singing *The Kielder Hunt* with superb brass accompaniment, and the monologue *The Bellingham Show*, which nobody does better. ("Which are the duck's eggs, and which are the drakes?"). And the finish of the show, his own composition, *The Hexham Mart*, with the cod auctioneers' patter, a fitting end to a magnificent production. He should be proud of that, despite the difficulties of production.

The North Sea Suite 1986

Two years later, the Cutty Sark Tall Ships' Race came to Newcastle for the first time. He must have thought "What could I do for this?" It would be *The North Sea Suite* doing a similar job for the Sea as for the Tyne. Geoff said "I could do it again if I have a band", and Johnny was anxious to continue this amalgam of folk song and brass. (Some of the foremost folkies in the land, Martin Carthy and John Kirkpatrick saw the same light in the form of *Brass Monkey* about the same time.) He and Geoff negotiated funding from *Northern* Arts, and managed to get the very prestigious Eveready Band for expenses. The band had been formed in 1910 as the Craghead Colliery Band, but unfortunately, 1968 saw Craghead Colliery being one of the first North East coal mines to close. However, many of the miners in the village found good jobs at the newly opened Eveready batteries factory in the nearby village of Tanfield Lea. Hence the band's name at the time, and although the factory closed down in 1993, the band carried on as the the Reg Vardy brass band, still to be seen at the Durham Gala in July. This time Johnny used the other two Ranters as musicians, and three singers including myself. This was an eye-opener for me, and certainly showed the difference between the cultures. Johnny had decided on the songs and tune to use, and Geoff had scored it for a top quality brass band. Now Johnny was not keen on practising, and turned up late one time. The band, of course, had been there for ages, all rehearsed, professional and raring to go. The bandmaster tore Johnny off a strip in front of the rest of us, exquisitely embarrassing, but necessary. It all came together well, was even better than *Tyne Valley* and was performed during Tall Ships' week in 1986 at what was then the University Theatre in Newcastle, now called Northern Stage. It was also recorded by Radio Newcastle and broadcast shortly afterward. Two things struck me about this experience. As a singer, being accompanied by quiet brass is fantastic – it takes all the effort out of it. The song I remember in particular is *I drew my ship into a harbour*, already a splendid tune. The other thing is that we only gave the one performance, as with *Tyne Valley*, and there was bound to be first night nerves. Certainly I made a couple of fluffs. With the effort that had gone into it by all concerned, it should have had more outings. As a postscript to this production, I listened again to the recording and was surprised by two items which I delivered but had completely forgotten about. One was a comic monologue, *The million ton tanker*, written by Jack Davitt (Ripyard Cuddling), but the other was a song written by Johnny especially for the show. Most of the theme had been about the past, so he brought it up to date with *The Roughneck Riggers* about the men who worked on the North Sea oil rigs then coming on stream. It had an original, catchy tune, and fine sentiments. Of course, things have moved on, so I added some verses and it is now in the Keelers' repertoire.

Outbye with dog

Chapter 6 Johnny the researcher

"JOHNNY HANDLE, a man who deserves capital letters."
Pete Coe

ALREADY STEEPED IN TWO ASPECTS OF LOCAL LIFE, THE PITS AND RURAL LIFE, when he took up folk song in the late fifties, Johnny, like any other Northeasterner, knew some local songs, if only thanks to the Catcheside Warrington books. However, as already mentioned, he found Bert Lloyd's *Come all you bold miners* an eye opener, and even with his busy life he still found time to learn as much as he could about the music of the area. So, although many found him a great entertainer and a comedian, the more discerning would also be impressed by his knowledge and ability to link songs and tunes to each other, and set them in the context of his own life. Not only that, by the mid-sixties he was already doing workshops in the area, and had organised the Tuesday sessions at the Bridge to include talks by such as Louis Killen and Forster Charlton. He tried getting people to appreciate local material, how to mix songs and tunes, and the fact that there are enough North East songs to do medleys. "If you want to play tunes, try the whistles". The work could be entertaining, but quite easy to do. At folk festivals, especially Whitby, he has done many different kinds of workshops and talks, frequently using material he has found in North East archives. He gave tailored advice to individuals, took real trouble, with a list of points to improve their playing without stretching them too far.

The region had by the 1990s had earned a reputation for being the foremost region of England for the quality and uniqueness of its traditional song and music. Not only that, the number and quality of its performers had ensured its prominence in the folk revival, centring, I would suggest, on the subject of this biography and his colleagues. However, there then started a process of the academisation of folk music, starting with the Newcastle Folk Music Degree course at Newcastle University. Alistair

Anderson we have already met and seen something of his career, but by then he was leading *Folkworks*, which for twelve years had run many workshops, summer schools and festivals to promote and encourage the furtherance of folk music. Ali was co-director with Ros Rigby, and they had allied themselves with the music department at the university to launch the first full degree in folk music in England. This was 2002, and the course continues to be an outstanding success story.

Johnny had had an early taste of research in the mid-sixties when he was doing his teaching course. On the course he had come across the Opies' books of children's songs, games, and rhymes, so when he came to do his thesis, he decided to research the area. So he would go round school playgrounds, recording what he heard, at first in the Dudley area he'd become familiar with in his pit days. He then compared what he had with the Opies' material, and Cramlington with "the toon". In schools, when he talked to the teachers, they'd say "No, they don't do hopscotch, skipping, and that". But when he went into a playground, the kids were doing exactly that. He then "borrowed the class" for the morning and kids "couldn't get enough of it". Years later, in the eighties, he found at High Spen the same games happening. We agree it's still going on. I say "the playground has no technical gear, they fall back on the trad stuff." He says "it was just like oral tradition." Anyway, his external examiner was very interested, but Johnny found a bit of a hitch in passing the course. His accent was considered "too broad", so he had to pass a speech test, being given a speech therapist.

Meanwhile, while he was researching the kids' songs, the North East rep of EFDSS, Graham Binless, saw that the time was ripe for folk music in the area to be a bit more organised, and in December of 1966 set up the North East Folk Federation, always known simply as "The Fed". Chaired by Tony Wilson, with Pete Elliott and Jim Irvine as joint secretaries, the Fed was set up to promote folk music in the wider North East, and had people from the whole region on the committee. After organizing two Jack Elliott memorial concerts and his posthumous LP, The Fed grew from strength to strength, taking over the fledgling Hexham Festival, organising workshops, and eventually having a major involvement in the Newcastle Festival of the early seventies. The organization then turned its attention to research, purchasing a tape recorder, an ex-BBC Uher portable machine which was then the state of the art, and sent people such as Johnny, Tony Wilson, Phil Ranson, and Pete and Reece Elliott off to find music and songs amongst ordinary people.

Johnny was too busy to have a major role in the Fed, but had been fascinated by the older people of the area, who were still congregating in peoples' homes and in particular the Alnwick Gathering, started in the 1940s by the Alnwick Pipers' Society, with an obvious concentration on Northumbrian pipes. Thus the pipes culture and repertoire were being maintained in north Northumberland well before the second folk revival got going in Newcastle in the late fifties. So after his adoption of folk music, he started to explore the region. This was greatly helped by his being a part-time warden for the National Park, going up at weekends on his motorbike, camping at Alwinton, with a warden's beat between there and Elsdon. As anybody from the North East will tell you, there can scarcely be a better area for scenery, characters, and music. Amongst others, it was in this period he met the piper Joe Hutton, Haltwhistle fiddler George Hepple, John Armstrong of Carrick, also a fiddler, as well as a fearsome character, and singer Jimmy White.

He waxes lyrical about Jimmy, a character and shepherd about whom there are so many stories. One will suffice. Like many a shepherd working for the big landowners, he was allowed to have a few sheep for himself, and some good dogs, which allowed him to bank money. One day he goes to the mart at Kelso, just over the border, and buys a prize ram for a large amount of money. As he did not drive, how would he get the beast back to Elsdon forty miles away? The solution was to hire a taxi, which he duly did (think of the mess!). Jimmy had a number of songs, including *The dosin' of the hoggs,* (young sheep) and *The Canny Shepherd Laddie of the hills.* He also had strong views about accordion playing, so on one of Johnny's visits, he struggled up to the loft, brought down an ancient wind-up gramophone, and played a 78 rpm record of Will Starr, the great Scottish accordion player. "That's how to play the instrument" said singer Jimmy – you could not argue. Jimmy was brimming over with one-liners. On one occasion, there was a goose in the garden with a twisted neck "Aye, tried to ring its neck last Christmas, but aa made a baals of it". Yes he'd had a wife way back, but "she didna tak tiv it, so I put her on the bus and sent her back tiv hor mither". When I point out that Johnny himself had absorbed a lot of Jimmy's approach to story-telling, with the exaggerated Northumbrian dialect, he does not disagree.

Article about Jimmy by Johnny

Bryce Anderson of the Cheviot Ranters band gave him a few singer contacts, but many of them sang material outside the folk genre, like Dennis Weatherly. This reminds me of the collectors from the first revival, such as Lucy Broadwood and Cecil Sharp, who had their own agenda as to which songs their sources should sing for them. Mind you they had a different agenda from Johnny. They would not, I suspect, have been interested in *The Dosin' of the Hoggs*. When I point out my well-banged drum of "People from outside the area wanted the music but not the songs" Johnny says "they've died out".

So, when Johnny heard about the Fed recording project, he was very keen to be involved, though how he found the time beats me. His interest in north Northumberland chimed well with the others in the group, particularly Pete Elliott, who was interested in urban areas of Tyneside, recording the family, and visiting old peoples' homes in north Durham, Johnny worked with Tony Wilson to interview some important source people from the rural areas. George Hepple was outgoing, and a good teacher, tutoring Gillian Yellop who went on to win the All Scottish Fiddle Championships. Yet another Johnny story emerges. Gillian's dad was a policeman at Haltwhistle, and was very keen on the Scottish stuff, taping *Take the Floor* every week. *Take the Floor* is a BBC Scotland Saturday night programme of Scottish dance music, to which Johnny often listened. He liked to listen to tapes of the programme on his daily commute to and from the School. "It certainly gave me a confidence in tune selection and composing, and helped me to improve my accordion style. The MC, Robbie Shepherd, was great". When he met the policeman in the street, they'd discuss the programme, and Johnny would occasionally be invited into the police station to hear recordings. David Reay, a piper and part owner of the Bardon Mill Pottery, was another enthusiast of the programme, who would meet up with Johnny at the Bowes pub on a Monday and have a natter. "David was a man of the valley, knew where the salmon spawned, and the history of everybody, especially musicians".

With George Hepple, they not only recorded him playing tunes, but interviewed him describing musical life in the area, including such topics as the Bellingham Show, Clipping Day, and dance styles. One of the other musician recorded by Johnny and Tony was Billy Conroy, ex-miner and whistle player who lived in Ashington. These recordings form an invaluable part of the North East musical heritage, making a notable contribution to both the Anthology and the FARNE project to be discussed next. [There is a fuller account of the Fed's activities in my book *The Elliotts of Birtley*, Herron Books (2008)]. In the early seventies, Topic Records were interested in seeing how many "source musician" were still playing, and asked Johnny for his opinion about it. Accordingly, Tony Engle and Tony Wilson recorded many musicians which led to the *Bonny North Tyne* LP, including Billy Atkinson, Joe Hutton, John Armstrong, Billy Conroy, and George Hepple and Donald Ridley.

Many of the people Johnny met in his collecting days did not appear on recordings, but did provide interesting stories of course. Jimmy Pallister was a fiddle player who worked as a blacksmith at Cambo. He played in many bands in the area, knew lots of tunes and other players. People would call into the smithy, take the fiddle off the wall, and play a few tunes while Jimmy was adjusting his hearth. One day, Johnny said he ought to have a phone, at which Jimmy recounted the time he'd had one. Part of the craft of his job was judging just when the heated steel was ready for repair, which was down to the exact colour ("sort of purple round the edges"). He was in the middle of repairing one of his own ploughs, which had lasted thirty years, when the phone went and he dropped the job to answer it. When he returned, the time had passed, and he was forced to make a new plough. That day he removed the phone and had never had one thereafter. Johnny also remembers the Alwinton postman, another fiddle player, who would play in the pub with his dog beside him which was wearing his master's hat with his pipe in its mouth. People took photos! At which point Johnny says "Stories? I could go on. We'd be here from now till bedtime".

The Northumbria Anthology
Meanwhile, Johnny had been engaged in another academic development. Having just retired from teaching, in 2000, he saw a job advertised in the paper for a full-time researcher to work on a collection of songs and poems from the North East of England, financed by a Heritage lottery grant. The project was the brainchild of Brian Mawson, who with his wife Helen had for many years operated Mawson & Wareham. This not-for-profit company had been actively promoting all aspects of North

East culture, in particular by producing CDs and DVDs. In addition to Brian the committee responsible for the project had members from the University Music Department, Gateshead Arts, the North East Museum service, and Alistair Anderson from Folkworks. This meant of course a significant overlap with the degree course, and gave it academic authority.

Johnny had no time to do any collecting himself, but compiled an extensive amount of vernacular material, mainly from the 19th and early 20th Centuries. From his initial base of over 3000 titles, almost 500 songs were recorded in a variety of musical styles. These range from the orchestral arrangements of David Haslam (Northern Sinfonia) to music hall, folk, and rock. Brian Mawson has insisted in all his projects in involving as wide a range of musical cultures as possible. Hence on the twenty CDs which were issued, there are performances from Johnny, Bob Fox, and Benny Graham, but also Bryan Ferry, Mark Knopfler, Sting, Jimmy Nail, as well as Lindisfarne, and Billy Mitchell. There were also classical people such as Sir Thomas Allen, Graeme Danby and Claire Rutter alongside actors Tim Healy, Alun Armstrong, Kevin Whately, and others. David Haslam of Northern Sinfonia, and Owen Brannigan also contributed.

Johnny divided the North East into fifteen geographical zones, from Tweed to Tees, digging into printed sources, and the records of collectors, including recent ones such as John Gall then at Beamish Museum, and the Folk Federation collecting initiative previously mentioned. The job was to research songs and poetry, not tunes. He knew he could get enough from three-quarters of the region, but was taking a bit of a gamble on some others. They might not have anything worth collecting. For example, Teesside only came into being in the mid-1800s due to its very rapid industrialisation, quite different from the rest of the region. However, the rural areas of North Yorkshire and Weardale provided recitations, and songs and poems from a group of naturalists. There was a lead miner who wrote songs, as well as newspapers and libraries. This was a great re-skilling exercise for him, aged 65. He was given a Dell computer and talks about photocopying difficulties. Well, our generation has had to learn everything on the hoof. If a poem was worth it, and had a song format, he'd put a tune to it. I estimate that as many as forty items fall into this category. This alone would have daunted most of us, but for him such an exercise seems almost routine. Brian Mawson already had recordings copyrighted of people like Owen Brannigan and Dennis Weatherly, and these went on to the CDs direct. When I ask about how much time it took, Johnny replies "A lot. I was getting paid, it was a job, But, a dream job!"

As Johnny says, "Although I didn't always agree with his choice of artists to perform the material, we worked well enough together over the three years". I think I agree with Brian's approach for this kind of project. Not a criticism of Johnny, but sometimes folk people forget that folk songs originated with working people, they are not the chattels of academics to lay down the law and promote pedantry. He has enormous energy, as we have seen, but the mechanics of this could be frustrating. For instance, each time he had the material selected for a sub-region, he had to submit cassettes and words to every member of the committee. It was agreed that this was counter-productive so eventually it was him, Brian, and the Professor of Music who decided on the content. As Brian says on his website: "Imagine Johnny fitting all this into his crowded schedule, and coming out with great success. Although his knowledge of local culture was already prodigious, the project expanded this, surely making him the most learned of people in this area, in addition to his musical talents. Lesser men would have balked at the task. Hats off!"[1] Two Radio Four programmes were made about the Anthology, with Johnny explaining the project and illustrating this with musical examples. They were broadcast in July 2002, entitled *Geordie Black*. He was kept busy afterwards replying to interested listeners from all over Britain and Europe. Some even sent previously undiscovered documents relating to the area.

Was the project a success? Copies were given to all universities and sixth form colleges, who used it as an educational resource. Junior schools were selected, for which he would make a package of songs from their area and elsewhere, a prodigious amount of work. However, the education committees were not interested. He'd already prepared booklets ready for launch, so Brian issued two sampler CDs and wanted to issue them commercially. Then he got interested in DVDs, so made one using the anthology material, including two verses of Chevy Chase with Johnny at Bellingham Cricket club filmed by helicopter. (Brian

1 http://www.northumbriaanthology.com

is never short of ideas, and has lots of connections.) Another aspect of Johnny's "re-skilling" was the use of computer software to "convert recordings to dots, and pass them on to the classical people on the project. I found it difficult to hold my tongue so I ended up telling professional opera singers how to do it". He says they were very good about it, but I'd love to have witnessed that scene. The problem with the project was that potential folkie buyers were put off by what he calls "the different approach" and classical buffs didn't want to hear folk songs. The project for me illustrates the many divergent musical cultures we have in this country. Thus opera, classical, musicals, jazz, and folk each attract a certain type of person, both performer and audience, who concentrate on that to the exclusion of the rest. Moreover, modern and traditional jazz seem poles apart, and in folk, there are three distinct groups, song, music, and dance. I participate in the first two, but very few other people do so. There have been several memorable evenings where all aspects of folk are on display, but they are rare, despite many attempts by individuals to promote or even impose togetherness. Yes, of course, there are exceptions. Johnny exempts Brannigan from his comments. Dave Brocksop, a Geordie folkie, who bought the collection, commented "You've got the words, you've got the tune, but you can sing it any way you like". My instincts favour Dave, and also Brian Mawson, for his valiant attempts to break down these barriers. The Northumbria Anthology continues as a non-profit charity, and Brian still has hopes to bring out more CDs and DVDs of local material.

FARNE

Folk Archive Resource North East (FARNE) was a project mounted by Gateshead Council, Newcastle University, and Sage Gateshead with financial support from the New Opportunities Fund. 2004 was an exciting time for folk music in the North East, with Sage Gateshead, incorporating *Folkworks*, looking forward to the opening of the magnificent music centre on the banks of the Tyne later that year, and lots of other pioneering ideas. The project placed on the web an extraordinary range of North East music and song by digitising original collections and manuscripts from as early as 1694 to the late 20th century. Here is an extract from my review of the project for *Living Tradition* magazine:

"FARNE has placed on the web an extraordinary range of Northumbrian music and song by digitising original collections and manuscripts from as early as 1694 to the late 20th century. What we see on the screen (and can print off a copy) is the original material used in famous North East publications like Bell's *Rhymes of Northern Bards* and *The Northumbrian Minstrelsey* alongside material which never got published, but is of equal importance. The search engine and presentation is of the very highest quality and designed to make life as easy as possible for both the casual browser and the serious researcher. There is an enormous amount of material in these collections, but a finite budget and timescale was available to produce the site. Hence the chief problem for the steering group was selection. There was also the need to add notes to the display (the digitisers call this "metadata", a term we'll all need to be familiar with in the future). Fortunately this was in the very safe hands of Johnny Handle for the songs and Matt Seattle for the music, and you'll be able to follow up the missing material for yourself."

Johnny applied for the post of researcher as with the *Anthology*, and with that experience got the new job. As he says "For me, this was a natural evolution from the research for the *Anthology*, although much more detail on the historical side was needed. I had much help from the Gateshead Librarians, which let me make the website into a fuller source for all levels of interest." However, he did not think he had the time to do all the work, so he concentrated on songs, while Matt Seattle covered the tunes. Whereas the *Anthology* project had meant a significant upgrading of his library research skills, FARNE meant dealing with the new digitisation process, as well as computers. There were two professional programmers actually inputting the data, who would write the notes based on Johnny's direction to the sources, and he would check it. The site has many audio recordings, from the FED project, Beamish Museum, and private material. As described earlier in this chapter, Johnny had spent some time recording various performers in Northumberland. No fewer than ninety-two items on FARNE were contributed by him.

Although I could criticise the balance of song and music, particularly the song recordings, which seem limited almost entirely to the Elliott family, and a search engine which by today's standards seems to need an upgrade, the quality of the notes and provenance for each article remain superb for both tunes and songs. At the time of writing, I hear that there is to be an update of FARNE, which will assumedly address some of these issues, and hopefully include the Edwardian recordings of many Tyneside songs researched by Ray Stevenson, material from the twenties and thirties, as well as *Wotcheor Geordie* from the fifties. Needless to say, Johnny has several ideas for any further development.

Folkworks

The *Folkworks* project has been mentioned previously, and it can be no surpise that Johnny was an active participant in this. The concept of combining the talents of teachers and musicians throughout the region involved expertise in song, music and dance. There were also skills needed in communication of ideas. Johnny fitted the bill in most of these situations and was employed from 1994 to 2008 to join the teams in primary schools in Hartlepool, Seaham, Sunderland, Gateshead, Newcastle and North Tyneside. Traditional material was linked with new compositions by the pupils. Productions were organised to include these, in cooperation with school staff. Recordings of songs and dances were distributed to teachers, so that they could rehearse at times convenient to the curriculum demands. Highlights of these visits produced some memorable creations. *The Horrible Troll* (Southwick) and *The Pets' Song* (Crookhill) continue to be popular amongst many children, and *The Ship Dance* (Wallsend) had a wonderful circle formation, which could use up a whole class of thirty pupils. A two-year project, *Coal, Shipyards and Waggonways* based in North Tyneside culminated in a marvellous concert in Hall One at the Sage, Gateshead with over a thousand pupils enjoying the massed singing and dancing. As Johnny says "Each one a Star!"

The Composers' Club

In 2002, Johnny set up a series of original nights, arising from the research he was doing for the *Northumbrian* Anthology described above. He wanted to give people a chance to hear the songs. These

Alex Clough. George Welch. Raymond Reed. John Green. Henry Robson. Billy Pigg . Thomas Wilson . James Hill . Colin Bradford . Ron Angel Joe Wilson . Alistair Anderson . Tommy Armstrong . Fred Reed .Vin Garbutt.Alexander Barrass . Forster Charlton. Rowland Harrison. Ned Corvan. Willy Taylor. George Ridley . Robert Whinham. Jez Lowe J.P.Robson .Archie Dagg. Thomas Todd. Bobby Nunn.Tom Clough. William Mitford . Tom Carruthers. Jack Armstrong. Roy Hugman. Richard Grainger. Marshall Creswell. Eddie Pickford. Robert Allan Will Atkinson. Thomas Thompson. Billy Ballantine. Will Coombs. James Armstrong. Richard Butler. George Hepple. Robert Bolam. Billy Bell. James Anderson. Terry Common. Ron Purvis. Nick Short Joseph Skipsey. Peter Athey. Terry Conway. Lewis Proudlock.

Eric Boswell	
William Bowden	Wilfred Gibson
Edward Chicken	Richard Haswell
Richard Watson	Jack Davitt
Jim Moreland	William Dunbar
Billy Fane	Robin Dunn
James Weams	Alex Glasgow
Donald Ridley	Jock Purdon
Bert Draycott	Felix Burns
Harry Nelson	Alan Price
Katherine Tickell	Graham Dick
	Graeme Miles

THE COMPOSERS CLUB

Benny Graham. Chuck Fleming. George Mitchell. Allan Wood. Anne Lunen Cowan. Bryce Anderson. Johnny Handle. Barry Temple. Alan Fitzsimmonds.Dennis Telfer.John Harbottle.JudyDinning. Henry Brewis. Scott Dobson. Ted Elkins. Keith Gregson.James Horsley. Edna Scott. Jack Robson. Norman Turnbull.John Peacock. Brian Jaques. Dick Murray. Catcheside Warrington. Bill Hume. Norman Foster. Tom Patterson . Henry Pearson. Ellen Thompson. HarryWaine. RalphDowey. MaryWade. R.J.Wilkinson. John Shield. Thomas Doubleday.

ALL LOCAL POETS, SONGWRITERS AND TUNE WRITERS FROM THE NORTH EAST OF ENGLAND. 1780-2002. CELEBRATE THEIR WORK EVERY MONTH AT THE BRIDGE HOTEL.

Perhaps you have a favourite, or your own new compositions?

The Composers Club
At the Bridge Hotel, Newcastle
Wednesday June 9th

Brian Watson
Tyneside Singer

also
The High Level Ranters
And Benny Graham
8pm £3

were run once a month at the Bridge Hotel, concentrating on a particular songwriter, or a group. Not only were the great music hall composers of the nineteenth century covered, but a night was accorded to such contemporary composers Ed Pickford, Terry Conway, and Graeme Miles. In doing these, he used a wide range of local singers and musicians, including Robin Dunn, Ray Fisher & Chris Hendry, and Colin Bradford. Pete Scott and Alan Fitzsimmons did a Joe Wilson night, there was a pipers' night with Chris Ormston, and a Ned Corvan night with Keith Gregson. He did nights on James Hill, Whinham, Rowland Harrison, even Teesdale composers. Once he'd run through the more obvious and local ones, he set up a "Lanky Neet", and asked me to be involved. A few days before the event, I rang him and asked who else was involved. "Nobody" was the reply "It's just ye. Two forty-fives. OK?" Well, I'd always done quite a few Lancashire songs, later extending to some of the Marriott Edgar monologues about the Ramsbottom family, along with some George Formby and other comic bits and pieces, but I fell well short of the required time. As a last resort, I resorted to Lancashire dialect poetry, which I'd not done before. It was traditional to do these items by reading off the printed page, which I found essential. Also, though much of the genre was maudlin, sentimental stuff, there were gems amongst them. So, Ned Waugh, Sam Laycock, and Ammon

Wrigley from the old days were included, along with present day dialect poet Scowie (Keith Scowcroft from Bolton). Not only that, but the inclusion of these helped to qualify the event as a night of "composers' items", which I'd been worried about. So much so that on the night I provided real genuine Bury black pudding together with parkin made by myself. Didn't half go down well. Anyway, despite feeling a bit nervous about qualifying for such a night, that helped enormously, and I really enjoyed it. I felt that despite me not being a composer, it had the same mood as all the other nights Johnny had run in the series. This was like many another occasion I've shared a stage with him. You could just lean on him. I've only twice seen him scared of an occasion, but they'll keep for elsewhere in the book.

He is self-critical about plugging the Composers' club, saying that people weren't interested in the academic approach. I think, even at his most academic, he is more interesting than most people are when trying to entertain. When I asked him about the thinking behind the project, he said he thought the folk clubs were becoming "samey", more like singarounds. There were so many songs where the composer was known, especially on Tyneside, but there was more to it than Wilson and Ridley. Was it an educational mission? He resists the term, but wants people to know more and attach it to their material. It had to be presented in an informative, but entertaining light. Isn't that always the case with him, and don't you always learn? He wanted people to say "This is great, why didn't we know this? It's good stuff. This is about history I'm interested in". He wonders if he's a bit of an anorak. I say nobody would have thought that for a minute. He hands me a complete file of handouts over three years of operation. Why do you think it a failure? "Audiences dwindled. "Perhaps I was not adept at the publicity angle. It had run its course. It could have had better audiences." I profoundly disagree. I admit I didn't attend every night, but the ones I did were a great success.

Johnny does not rate himself highly as a researcher, and will probably be surprised to find a chapter of this title. There may be others who are professional historians who dig deeper into social history, but, I can think of nobody who knows more about North East song and music than him, and the way he has gone about this learning is of the highest professionalism.

Chapter 7. The Songs

"Goin' to the mine"

JOHNNY'S WEBSITE LISTS 132 SONGS AND 317 TUNES. A PRODIGIOUS CREATIVE output worthy of a more extensive study than this work will allow, but let us make a start. It is hardly surprising that one or two have been forgotten. Also, I was aware that he had written a number of recitations which are apparently not listed. At the time of writing, there are 101 songs and 37 recitations. As a result, I will treat them in separate chapters. Since he is best known for his songs, and they by and large started first, this chapter deals with them.

What was it that got him started on these creations? The reasons are refreshingly honest. At the start, he was doing local songs from books, after the American stuff, and even what he calls "pooks of hay songs", his own term for those collected in the south by Sharp *et.al.* He mentions the value of what Peter Kennedy had collected and issued on record. Johnny was very generous with giving other people the words of songs, and of course they started singing them. What he found was that there were gaps in these songs in terms of their coverage of everyday life, so he set about filling these gaps, using his own experience. Once he started composing, there was no stopping him, and although he has continued with the established or traditional North East music, his own creations have featured increasingly prominently on his gigs. I suppose the prolific composers in our revival have been much the same. I'm thinking of Jez Lowe, Terry Conway and the like locally. Ed Pickford has only ever done his own songs. His main inspiration was Matt McGinn, who did just that – "That's what I want to do". That's why Ed took that path, and in the next breath he asks "Why did Johnny take his path?" I draw the conclusion that is what songwriters do. Bob Dylan, the Beatles, and The Stones come to mind at this point. The first albums included songs that reflected their early interests, but thereafter it was their own stuff. When I asked him about his 1980 song, *Going to the Mine*, one of his most popular songs, he reveals that it is based on a 1954 poem. Wow! It seems that before his first song creation, he wrote "bits and pieces", starting with *Guard Yer Man Well*, and the chorus of *The Collier Lad*. In the Tyneside jazz scene of the fifties, he kept these things quiet. We are talking future pit songs here of course, and much of his "scratchings" were mining related. So, whilst his songs cover a very wide range of subject and mood, let us start by looking at his pit songs.

Pit Songs

It was a bit of a shock for his family, him leaving Heaton Grammar to go down the pit rather than following the academic course his father had planned for him. His translation of some of the pitmen's vernacular was a challenge, but essential as they were frequently used as work instructions. These things were often about dangers underground and ways to avoid them. As discussed earlier in this book, his earlier songs were inspired by reading the first edition of Lloyd's *Come All Ye Bold Miners*, and his increasing knowledge of real life down the pit in his day job.

Farewell to the Monty, his very first song, is a nostalgic look back on the Montague Colliery at West Denton, regretting its closing, despite its' having been a tough one. So supportive is the tune of the sentiment, that it became an instant hit in the burgeoning folk revival of the early 1960s, far beyond Tyneside. The Montague colliery was well within the boundaries of Newcastle, had been going since the 1700s, and was still a productive colliery in the late fifties. Pit closures were rare then, and the event attracted a lot of interest, including local TV. This was 1958, when Johnny and Louis were still doing their spot at the jazz club, when Tyne Tees TV asked Louis for a song about pit closure. They hadn't got one so Louis said "Ye write one." So Johnny, who had been in the Montague as part of his apprenticeship, obliged. The splendid, evocative tune came from an Irish song which got modified by Louis to suit his own singing style. Given the chance, once again Johnny will talk for considerable periods of time about the technical developments in mining. "They had the ninety-fathom dyke, so they put a drift through – when they hit it, there is this lovely four foot Beaumont [a major coal seam]. Very saveable. It was called horizon mining, very advanced for the time. It kept going and going." He has incredible recall of the detail. In fact, he is very academic, despite being so self-deprecating on occasions, which is often but not always tongue in cheek. Anyway, the NCB decided that the cost of construction of a separate coal washery meant that the whole complex had to close. There are many people even today who regard it as his best song.

Within the next year or so Johnny wrote three songs which seem to be a bit of an antidote to the previous song, being cheery evocations of the happy go lucky young pitman in the good times, and perhaps reflect his own disposition at the time. These are **The Collier Lad**, about a team of handfillers at Dudley colliery, who always seemed to have more swagger than the other workers, **Stottin Doon the Waal**, a typical pit lad's Friday night out in Wallsend, including a visit to the pub (*The Penny Wet*) and the dance (Memorial Hall), and **Durham Big Meeting Day**, which vividly describes the unique atmosphere of the Miners' Gala. See the Appendix for Johnny's account of the first of these. **My Gaffer's Bait** is a comic tragedy describing a real event where he managed to lose his boss's lunch, an unpardonable sin in any walk of life, and definitely in a pit. **The Trepanner Song** and the recitation *The Abandoned Mine* were composed for the Centre 42 visit he made to the Nottingham coalfield described in Chapter 3. When I ask about *The Trepanner Song*, which I hadn't heard of, he gives me a short lecture on this device, which had greatly increased the efficiency of digging out the coal, was the "Wonder of the age" in the modern midland coalfields, and which eventually came to the North East. When he sings a bit, I realise that I have heard him do it after all. And I thought it was all about drilling into somebody's skull! Three more pit songs followed in the 1960s. **Dust** is what it sounds like – miserable conditions down below, leading to premature ageing and early death for many miners. A reflective performance, as with *Monty*. This was 1964, and he recalls some discussion with Eddy Pickford about writing a song for Jack Elliott, who was suffering from the effects of these conditions. So, Johnny wrote *Dust,* and Eddy wrote *Aa Cud Hew*, one of his most popular songs. It was about this time that the NCB started to do something about the problem. Too late for Jack Elliott, who not long after died of lung cancer.

FAREWELL TO THE MONTY

For man-y long years now the pit's done its best And
sets have rolled out of flats North, East and West And
all of the ru-mours that clos-in' was due Have
all been put down for a—las it is true.

A meeting was held to discuss the affair
And the Manager said to us, right then and there,
"We'll have one last go before this pit is done
To show a good profit on each single ton."

But though profits were made, though the stock's pilin' high
The Coal Board decided the pit has to die
And as output gans doon we get transferred away
Te pits te the South for the rest of wer days.

A've filled in the Fan Pit, a'ave cut in the Seam,
In the Newbiggin Beaumont, since aa was thirteen.
A'ave worked at the Sections and in the Main Coal
It's hot doon the Monty, she's a dorty black hole.

So farewell te ye Monty and aa knaa ye roads well
And ye work it's been good and yer work it's been hell.
Ne mair te yer dorty owld heap will aa come
For yer workin' is finished, and yer life it is done.

From the Johnny Handle Songbook

A COLLIER BRIG ON THE EASTERN SHORE

We load her up in Blyth, boys, they've al-ways coal in store   Low main from Nor-

thum-ber-land on the Coll-ier Brigs on the East-ern Shore·   And it's

past the Tyne and Hart-le-pools, round Flam-bro' Head once more   The

Geor-die lads is off to sea on the Coll-ier Brigs on the East-ern Shore.

CHORUS:

Though the sea be rough or smooth to Lon-don we will go   with

Geor-die coal fast down in the hold ; A

Coll- ier Brig on the East-ern Shore.

And when we'd get to Tilbury the watchman he would roar,
"Send news to town, the Geordies come, the Collier Brigs on the Eastern Shore."
We've coaled in sailing ships, been wrecked and sunk before
But wreckers or pirates canna stop the Collier Brigs on the Eastern Shore.

Aave sailed the seas around the world, aave seen ports by the score
But the hardest seas we ever shipped was the London run on the Eastern Shore.
But it's grand te caal in home, hinny, and see the bairns once more
So aave packed up ocean cargoes now, for the Collier Brigs on the Eastern Shore.

London's greatly altered now, bright lights and sights galore,
They still depend on Geordie coal, from the Collier Boats on the Eastern Shore.
And now the lighthouse is in sight we'll make the taverns roar,
It's many's the pint we'll have tonight, the stottin' lads on the Eastern Shore.

Collier Brig from the Johnny Handle Songbook

Much of the coal output from the North East was destined for London, and a vigorous trade built up, involving strongly built vessels called "Collier brigs", celebrated in the lively *A Collier Brig on the Eastern Shore* which was regularly sung by both Johnny and Louis. He took some relish in telling me a short story about how the song came about. "After delivering a roll of mine plans to the Blyth surveyor's office, I chanced upon a pub for refreshment. There I encountered a monthly social gathering of retired collier brig crews. Many of them had ancestors working the same London run in the days of sail. The following month I presented them with this song, which was approved. I missed two buses back to the town, cos the crack was so good" This had the benefit of great timing, since ten years later, these men would have been no longer there. So many traditional trades were disappearing during those times.

The seventies, eighties, and nineties found him putting pen to paper on many diverse subjects, and of pit songs there were few. However, two of his best songs arose in this period, both based on some earlier "scratchings". I refer to his earlier poems, later converted into songs. *Going to the Mine* is an evocative song about life in a pit village when there was still a pit, done to a great tune, and taken up by many local singers in the North East and further afield. I was brought up just outside Manchester in the forties and fifties, in an area of industrial decline, and both this song and *Monty* take me back there instantly. The other song is *Guard Yer Man Weel,* about the miner's wife at home all day worrying whether her man will return. Best sung by Johnny's wife Christine Hendry, but I could not resist it, and so sing it solo and with the Keelers. Following his much earlier song about the Durham Gala, in 2002 he wrote *The Banner Song*, a brief history of the centuries-old struggle of miners to improve their lot, and the song has become an anthem amongst North East folkies. The last pit in Durham closed many years ago, and now there are none in the UK. And yet the gala lives on, still taking up to five hours for the parade, with its brass bands and banners, to wind its way through the narrow streets of the old city. No doubt very different from the "aad days", it is still a splendid day out for everybody. For some years now, these have included a group of folkies who do not have a brass band, but a folk band led by Jim Bainbridge, carrying the "Cotia" banner so much part of the Elliotts of Birtley, and still including Doreen Elliott and husband Bryan Henderson, both well into their eighties.

It was inevitable that mining would feature strongly in his songwriting, and the second edition of *Come All Ye bold Miners* in 1978 included three of his songs. There was nobody better qualified to do this, but it has to be stressed that he was among a group of highly talented composers, all writing splendid songs about the pits, including Jock Purdon, a Glasgow Bevin Boy sent to Cotia pit in Birtley in World War 2, and a stalwart of the Elliotts' club, and Ed Pickford, Alex Glasgow, and Jez Lowe, all from North East mining families. The quality of all their songs is strikingly high, and regularly evokes very emotional reactions by audiences. There were many pits elsewhere in Britain, of course, but other regions did not appear to sing songs about them. Even in recent years Johnny has continued to add to his tally of pit songs. **Under the Fields of Heaton** was commissioned as part of a lottery sponsored project to commemorate the 1815 disaster. It was sung at various events over the 2015-16 year, and recorded for a CD with other various artists performing mining songs. Quite a bit of work went into the writing. He used two melodies, a single verse at the beginning and end, and then a narrative set of verses. The same idea was used in the Trepanner song, starting with the slow "pick, pick, pick", and then gearing up with a percussive melody like the machine. So, a total of about twenty pit songs out of the ninety-nine, with a wide range of subject and style.

Local Songs

We have seen how Johnny started his songwriting career with songs about mining, but he was by no means restricted in his subject matter. His next subject as a writer was the Tyneside environment in which he lived. The first foray was **The Day We Went to the Coast,** which is a jolly song about a family trip, probably to Cullercoats, which featured the customary heavy downpours, and burying his father in the sand. It's pure music hall, very jolly, entertaining, and he usually does it with superb piano accompaniment. Echoes here of a previous North East songwriter, Tommy Armstrong, with his *Wor Nanny's a 'Mazor.* One of the many songs Johnny wrote early in his career, which he still does, enjoys doing, and which always goes down well.

We buried me father at the coast,
An forgot to pull him oot.

That song was composed in 1960, and much later he came back on the same theme with *Come to the Briny Ocean,* a recitation discussed in the next chapter.

The Tynemouth Volunteer Life Brigade is a jolly, very popular song he wrote in 1977 in celebration of an outfit at the coast which is very nearly unique. Tynemouth was the first of a large number of such brigades nationally. It followed a 1864 incident involving a series of shipwrecks on the shoreline in which crew members perished, watched by spectators ashore who were powerless to help. A meeting was held to discuss the matter, and over 100 volunteers signed up to do something about it, i.e. set up a shore rescue outfit. Other brigades soon followed nationwide, often founded in similar circumstances and modelled along the lines of Tynemouth's example.

It's the Tynemouth Volunteer life brigade
They're the masters, aye the masters of their trade
They can work their breeches buoy like it was a little toy,
That's the Tynemouth Volunteer Life Brigade

The breeches buoy was the classic device which was used in exactly the situation described above whereby people could be lifted from a foundering ship close to the shoreline. The Black Middens are a group of rocks in Tynemouth harbour upon which many a ship has foundered. The Watch House, a clapboard construction which is Grade II listed, is a delight, and has hosted many a folk night over the years. Johnny's often comic salutation is to a noble outfit, which is still active in coastal rescue, but is one of only three such institutions now left. The others are just across the river at South Shields, and down the coast at Sunderland.

Sunderland, as we saw in Chapter 3, was the place where he was involved with a film about shipbuilding by Philip Donnellan in 1961. Johnny created the music for this, and wrote two songs, **Sunderland Oak** and **Is There Owt Secure?** The town was at its height in the mid-1800s, building one-third of Britain's ships, but after the World War Two things had deteriorated. *Owt Secure* is cleverly constructed to deliver a different punchline for each verse:

Oh we've got cash in hand

He hangs around at home

An lads wi nowt tae dae

Aalthough it's very hard

And loved ones far astray

So Aa must mend an mak

Aye then what will we dae?

Is there another keel?

Oh is there owt secure?

It took another twenty-seven years before shipbuilding ended on the Wear. I used to work in Sunderland and passed the Austin & Pickersgill shipyard every morning. So sad to see the half dozen small cargo ships sitting in their sparkling red and white livery, which had been rejected by the Danes, who had commissioned the ships. What ignominy for a town with such an imposing history. Johnny still sings both songs regularly.

The Old Pubs, regretting the passing of the traditional pub, was commissioned by the BBC, as described in Chapter 3. But it was so well constructed, and so in tune with the spirit of the times, that it became one of his most popular songs. Although written for the programme, it is most definitely based on what was happening in his area. The experience led to him composing three others on the theme of pubs and drink. **Danny's, Drinkin' at your leisure,** and the recitation *Let Yer Man Out for a Pint* are gems of Tyneside culture to rival if not surpass the likes of Corvan and Wilson, those nineteenth-century predecessors of what Johnny was now presenting to Tyneside audiences, folk and non-folk.

> Get yoursel's to Danny's,
> Sup aal the beer you can
> Ten and a half for a pint of Scotch,
> Why, hinny man ye canna gan wrang

Danny was the landlord of the Golden Lion at Winlaton Mill. "Scotch" was the local "cooking bitter" and the price, 10.5 p (new pee) was about right for 1971, when he wrote the song. The pub, which was adjacent to the long dead NCB Derwenthaugh coking plant, is now much as it was, with the name "The Red Kite" noting the highly successful introduction of the birds into the area in the nineties. Although Johnny was of a middle-class background, the song so well illustrates how deeply he appreciated the working class culture of the North East.

He's Got Them on the Run, written in 1977, was another jolly chorus song, this time about a Tyneside personality, Brendan Foster. Brendan, a long distance runner who by then had several Olympic and Commonwealth medals, was from Gateshead, a Geordie through and through, with a very winning manner which later helped him inaugurate The Great North Run and become a media commentator on athletics. Johnny adopted the same approach as with *The Tynemouth Volunteer Life Brigade*, and it worked again. Catchiness our man could deliver in spades. Neither of these songs in my mind was his best song, but they'll always get an audience going, and celebrate Tyneside culture.

> He's got them on the run
> He's got them on the run
> Brendan is the champion,
> He's got them on the run

The Ballad of Jack Crawford. Crawford was a hero at the Battle of Camperdown in 1797. The story tells us that half way through the battle, a shell broke the top part of the British flagship *Venerable's* mast

CHORUS:- *Get yoursel's te Danny's*
  Sup aal the beer ye can,
  Ten and a half for a pint of scotch,
  Why, hinny, man, ye canna gan wrang.

Aa've supped 'Fed' at aal the clubs
Broon at the 'Penny Wet',
Cocktails at the posh 'Tork's Heed',
But Danny's is the best beer yet.

Ye might like owld black Guiness,
Soot and vinegar neat,
That's aal reet for Irishmen,
But Danny's can't be beat.

There's Tolly Cobbled, (or dish watter)
Tetley's and Cameron's te,
They taste like nitric acid,
And it's Danny's beer for me.

So follow the owld 'Blue Star', me lads,
Follow it through and through,
Caal at the leek trench, afterwards,
And see what it can do!
Words and music by Johnny Handle 1970

Danny's

94

and Admiral Duncan's flag fell to the deck. This could have had drastic consequences. The lowering of the Admiral's flag was an indication to the rest of the fleet to cease fire and withdraw from action. At which point the Dutch would have fallen upon them, assuming that the British Fleet had given up. Jack, a keelman from Sunderland, managed to climb the mast and restore the Admiral's flag, and the British won the battle. Hence the phrase "nailing one's colours to the mast". Jack Crawford was acclaimed a national hero, fêted in London, received an audience with the King, and was granted a pension of £30 a year. Johnny tells the story more colourfully of course, "…it was a bit of a game…if the flag fell, they lost the game….it was the law….Jim'll tell ye…everybody knows that. Anyhow, Jack got the drawin pins out and kept climbing the mast… the local lads were not happy, they'd have to go home just as they were enjoying the battle 'I've only got one leg shot away, we're all right now…what'll we do with the cannonballs…. we'll give them to the bairns, we've run out of mints' (well they're hot you see like mints… so Jack Crawford kept nipping up the mast, cos he fancied the admiral like, just like Nelson and Hardy. Why says Duncan, 'we'll have to carry on, I was gannin to Majorca for my holidays, the wife'll not be happy…'" he continues of course in like vein, his accounts of history being always highly entertaining. Johnny wrote the song for the two-hundredth anniversary of the battle, celebrated in Sunderland by "The cooncil". He is not comfortable about seeing this sort of patter in print, but it's representative of what he's done over the years, so I've included it. Bob Fox's recording of this song has ensured that it has remained popular.

Rural Songs

Although as we have seen, he was reared in Newcastle, he was evacuated to Hexham during the war, where he experienced another environment, the Northumbrian countryside. So, when he moved to Winlaton Mill in 1969, he did the rural thing, growing leeks, chickens, eggs and spuds. Later, he moved outbye to Bardon Mill, where he set about rural life with typical zest, what with the banties, barring the geese, and planting apple trees. Despite commuting 30 miles each way to his day job on the outskirts of Newcastle, he was determined to make a stab at some sort of self-sufficiency. So, let us look at some of his rural songs.

He was already steeped in the countryside culture, so when foot and mouth struck in 1992, particularly in the north of England, Johnny felt compelled to write one of his most heartfelt songs, **The Butcher's in My Yard Now**. In his notes to his recording of the song, he says "This was the hardest song I have ever had to compose." I give it here in full, without further comment:

I heard they closed the shipyards down
Pits and steel works in the far off town
And now it's my turn to take me due
For the butcher's in my yard now.

In bye fields as the grass grows green
Crops of lambs like you've never seen
I've slept few hours this lambin through
But the butcher's in my yard now.

It's hard when you fight to bring forth life
Then comes the blow, the fear and strife
A carcass of each lamb and yowe
Oh the butcher's in my yard now.

Men in white overalls, Vets lined in grey
The army called on me yesterday
Funeral pyres, heaps of corpses grow
For the butcher's in my yard now.

There's Jack and Bob just doon the lane
Ne foot an mouth there but it's I'm to blame
They're next to loss their sheep and cows
Oh the butcher's in my yard now.

Silence in the medder, quiet the hill
Silence to the lifetime's work, the farmer's skill
They say start again, I wonder how
Oh the butcher's in my yard now.

Some think farming's just money they don't understand
About raisin stock and livin with the land
Aa'm still up at dawn but nae sheep or cows
Oh the butcher's left my yard now.

The Land Where the Fells Meet the Sky. A song written after hearing an interview with Hannah Hutton at Whitby Folk Week in 1999. Hannah is the widow of Joe Hutton, the border shepherd and one of the best Northumbrian pipers of recent times. She has a lovely voice in traditional style, but only started singing in public in later life, delivering a good number of Northumbrian rural songs, with what the Scots travellers would call "the coinneach", the knack of handling a traditional song in the right way. Johnny's comment after the talk was "A compelling story which spoke for all the hard working people in the wilder parts of Northumberland, and their traditions". The song he wrote was the title of a later CD of rural Northumbrian songs.

The Hexham Mart is one which was used in the Tyne Valley Suite described in Chapter 5. He says "I had toyed with it sometime before this, after seeing my neighbour, Arnold the Farmer, up at all hours, talking to him about farming (he was also a Scottish Country Dance band fan), and going to the Mart myself, eventually making a purchase. But it was finally put together for the show and has been one of my regularly used songs. It has been tested and approved by rural audiences, many of whom can visualise the procession of vehicles on Tuesdays into Hexham, particularly in the days when the Mart was at its old site, causing considerable congestion to town traffic. It is also an important song because of the dependence of farmers on the ebb and flow of prices, and the wait for payment for the nurture of their livestock. Another factor is the element of gambling on prices when buying. Bit like a rural stock exchange!".

Funny Songs

Many of the songs already discussed are of course humorous or at least lively, because of the nature of the man, but some of his funniest songs do not fit into any of the previous categories, so let us look at a couple now.

A song based on domestic experience shows his exquisite sense of comedy. ***Decoratin'*** is about the man being tyrannised by "the wife" to continually paint the house. (I have another musician friend in a similar situation, who refers to his wife's plans for him as "Schindler's List". He has only recently heard Johnny's song, and has vowed to do it as often as possible.)

A North Country Maiden. A delicious parody of *It's the same the whole world over*, composed by the great music hall comedian Billy Bennett in 1930, and transformed into a large number of obscene versions during World War 2. Johnny wrote this for yet another TV company in 1986 for a programme about the North-South divide. His version reverses the tale of the unfortunate maiden who turns out to be very fortunate indeed, with shades of *Grandfather's left me the old armchair.* The great entertainer and legendary jazz guitarist Diz Disley got it from Johnny, and had it in his repertoire for many years.

Canal Songs

In 1989 Johnny was doing a gig in the midlands, when he met Jeff Denison, a larger than life character who told him about his boat, and invited him over. When he arrived at Jeff's house at Ansty on the Oxford canal, he was expecting some sort of sailing boat on the driveway, so when he arrived he asked "Where's the boat?" "Up there" says Jeff, pointing to the canal embankment behind his house. There he saw the *Mary Anne*, Jeff's narrow boat. Now Johnny had as a lad had a week on the Llangollen canal, and had got the bug, but had enjoyed a somewhat busy life since that time. Jeff was in the habit of taking people on canal trips, which always seemed to end up moored close to a pub, where they would drink and sing, many landlords welcoming this. Jeff saw Johnny as being the perfect entertainer for this. "It's all about cups of tea, rum, and the maps in the cabin." says Johnny, and "it was like a dream". I said to him "You'd have done it for nowt?" He assured me that that was the case. "We'd get free beer, sometimes a free meal from the landlord" For the next four years he would have an Easter tour, mostly with Benny Graham, a sometime resident of the Bridge we met in Chapter 4, who was equally fascinated, and who could of course sing like a nightingale.

So these two entered the bar of the first pub, and started singing and playing, accompanying Jeff on his canal songs. Johnny found these a little unexciting, and by the next day he emerged with one of his best songs, **They're Coming Back to the Water**. "What a song!" says Benny. So much so, that this became the title track of a CD of canal songs made by Jeff and Benny in 1997. At least eight more songs and some tunes came out of these trips, the latter including a magnificent march *Braunston Locks*. *They're Coming Back to the Water* clearly reflected the national revitalisation of the extensive English canal system for leisure. The following year, he composed **The Easter Boatman**, where the very keen man with an unwilling wife hires a boat, and he's stuck on the canal with the kids all yammering away, and needs to be rescued. It's winter, well, late spring (he remembers Benny covered in snow). His wife is away down the towpath with the kids. He is rescued, however, by a boatload of students who just happened to be passing at the time.

Another pair of canal songs emerge from the tendency of extraneous materials to wrap themselves round the boat's propeller, and bring it to a juddering halt. This was not good news, since they had a timetable to keep –they might not get to the next pub! The job of freeing the binder twine, or whatever was stopping them moving, required a small, nimble man, neither of which adjectives could be honestly applied to either skipper Jeff, or fellow boatman Benny. So Johnny got the task of putting his hand in the freezing water, to try and free the stuff. He describes it as complete agony. So, he wrote the song, **The Tangled Prop**, in 1991 to describe this.

Most of Johnny's songs have original tunes, including some really great ones. They are all of course well suited to the mood of the song, but if he's stuck, he'll happily use an existing tune. So, **Down at the Pub on the Cut**, a jaunty little number as the title implies, he set to *Messing bout on the river*. No less than fourteen canal songs were created in this period. However, several years later he must have been cogitating about these canal songs, and came up with a kind of ultimate one. **The Ribbon in the Sky** describes an old man who can no longer take his boat out, so takes it to the cut to watch the other boats go by. Then they tell him they're going to open up the cut, and it's his path to heaven. It's the inland equivalent of Tennyson's *Crossing the bar*. Over to Johnny: "Waiting there with their traditional canal clothes on, with the stoves puffing away, the teapot's on the hob, and there's a handy pub close by. Boatman's heaven". More recently he penned a song called **The new**

Navigators in praise of the volunteers involved in canal restoration. The song has become popular at boating festivals and rallies.

In addition to his own songs, he has put tunes to many others. Where a song was included in a collection, it was frequently without a printed melody, or the tune was referred to by title only. However, he has written a number of tunes because the lyrics appealed to him. Early ones included Robert Nunn's *Drunken Bella Roy,* Alexander Barras's *The Putter,* Rowland Harrison's *Geordie Black,* and Tommy Armstrong's *The South Medomsley Strike*, now used regularly by other singers. The marriage of a good lyric and a carefully crafted tune can produce really outstanding gems, like *The Herd Laddie, The Mackerel Song, Here Dwells my Heart,* and Skipsey's *Collier Lad,* all enhanced when sung by Chris Hendry. *The Northumbrian Anthology* proved a fertile ground for more melody writing, and some fine songs were rescued.

One-off songs

Johnny spent much of his life as a teacher, mostly of children with special needs. Here is one song which relates to this:

Penny for the Guy. Way back in 1964, Tyne Tees TV wanted to involve school kids writing songs. Accordingly, Johnny obliged. As we have seen, he knows no fear. The children gave him the basic idea, and they wrote the song together. One of the students wanted to win the prize of a big box of fireworks as a prize for the fattest Guy. His granny said to use the old clippy mat in the shed. So they made a big fat guy which gave the chorus

> Penny for the Guy, penny for the guy
> He's stuffed with a clippy mat
> Bonfire neet will soon be here,
> So please put a penny in my old hat

He tells of the reaction of the TV producer, which he reproduces in his cod southern accent, the producer said "Oh Johnny, it just reeks of age. We must produce it with the children dancing around the mock-up fire with flashing lights. We simply must have them down here". So, off went the kids to the TV studios, where after doing the business they were allowed free range of the studios. As he tells the story, they really

PENNY FOR THE GUY

Card-board box-es, doors and a chair wood and papers ev-ery-where,

Planks and bran-ches pile up high-er, that's what gans on our bon-fire.

CHORUS:

Pen-ny for the Guy and pen-ny for the Guy, He's stuffed with a clip-py mat.

Bon-fire neet will soon be here so please put a pen-ny in my old hat.

Got the pennies saved up in a tin,
Shops have got their fireworks in,
Round and long and coloured bright,
Hurry up, hurry up, Guy Fawkes night.

Light the fire and roast the guy,
See the flames jump up in the sky,
Fireworks burnin' bonny and bright.
We've turned wer pennies te fiery lights.

Sparklers fizzle and bangers crack,
Mind out for that jumpingack.
Catherine wheel goes round on a pin,
Smoke and sparks and noisy din.

Ne fireworks left, it's time for bed.
The guy's been burnt and the fire is dead.
Wash off aal the muck and grime
But come round soon next Guy Fawkes time.

Penny for the Guy

went on the rampage, and some very nearly missed the bus home. Needless to say, this only happened once.

Johnny isn't given to party political stuff, but could make a social point very forcefully when he felt strongly about something. **Down in My Own Backyard** is a lovely song about a disabled young man living in a terraced house with a backyard, but still making the best of what he'd been given. It's given an exquisite tune, played in 1940s style.

> For ye don't know how hard in feels
> When you try to run but you're tied to wheels
> Soon I think my mind will heal
> When I'm down in my own backyard
> Down in my own backyard

As ever, there is a story attached to this song. This comes as a result of Johnny's association with Peter Cheeseman in Stoke. He was present when a national environment group gave an award to a disabled athlete, who'd turned his backyard into a superb garden. The neighbours were very impressed, so it caught on, and spread along the terrace in which the man lived. He was told about this by some of the man's friends, wrote the song, but alas never met him.

Hardly surprising then that he was persuaded to publish "The Johnny Handle Songbook" in 1975, which included several of the songs discussed above. That was due to Spin Publications, the publishing arm of The Spinners of Liverpool, the most successful folk group of the 1960s, certainly amongst the general public. However, that was long ago, and my many interviews with him in writing this book have caused him to consider a second edition. The same applies to his tunes, dealt later. Before that, let us turn to his recitations.

Chapter 8. The Recitations

"A good line of patter"

AS OUTLINED IN THE PREVIOUS CHAPTER, SOME OF JOHNNY'S SONGS STARTED out life as poems. *Wallsend Explosion* and *Going to the mine* are examples. He uses the terms poem and recitation interchangeably, but the widely used term monologue sometimes creeps in. There are traditional examples from the North East, such as the hilarious *Bellingham Show, The Tyneside Tattooist,* and the *Geordie Bible* stories, all of which are done to perfection by Johnny. But he is also a great admirer of the Lancashire monologues, and when Gary Hogg, a North East monologuist, recently started turning out North East stories in the same style, Johnny started doing some of them, including making a whole CD, *Gary Hogg's Fairly Truthful Tyneside Tales*. However, in the recitation stakes, he has been no slouch himself. Of 136 "songs" listed on his website, 37 are recitations. And I know of at least one other that's not listed, but that story will keep for now. Like his songs, the recitations cover the widest range, from comical to wistful to profound. Many of his ideas come from things "that happen to him", of which there are a great many, and there's always a story to go with them. Let us start with the funny ones.

Funny

Quite a few of these centre on domestic difficulties. The title of the first, **Let Yer Man Out for a pint**, makes the subject pretty clear and yes, is male chauvinism, but with tongue in cheek, and located firmly in Geordieland. What is more, it's a recitation with a chorus, which is worth giving here:

Let yer man out for a pint
It's a joy to be out in the night
And when he comes yem he'll do what he can
When he comes in from hevin' a pint

Another great creation is **A Good Line of Patter,** where the Chaplinesque lovable rogue uses his silver tongue to get out of the worst of scrapes. He describes this as "A handy skill in the entertainment business", a telling remark since he has developed many devices over the years for holding an audience's attention. He records that he wrote it on the way to a Ranters' gig, and that it was based on Shakespeare's *Seven Ages of Man*. It is most certainly autobiographical. Being at a loss for words is not one of his characteristics!

As we have already seen, many of his best creations are based on observing a one-off event. **The Failed Shepherd** is in this category. At Rothbury Folk Festival one year, he was sitting in the schoolroom, waiting to judge the next competition, when out of the window he saw a man trying to organise some sheep, but having some difficulties. "The shepherd and the dog were totally at a loss with each other. The sheep had their own mind made up". Before the next competition, he had composed the poem, and recited it to the audience when at last his turn came. They laughed out loud, for the man in question was very well known in the area for his lack of skill in that department.

This ability to compose quickly was a characteristic of his local TV appearances on a topic of the day described earlier, but is best demonstrated by a monologue that is not on his list. When I was doing gigs with him in the nineties, we got a regular gig at Otterburn Hall, for the librarians who were having their annual conference. No matter what time we got there, they were always over-running with some riveting lecture, so we had to hang around. The hall was somewhat run-down, elegantly seedy, but had a full-size snooker table in very good nick. So Chuck Fleming and I would enjoy ourselves for about an hour, not worried about how Johnny was passing time. As I began to realise, Johnny is a man who, faced with a vacuum, will always fill it productively. It was later, when we were playing that we found out what. He delivered a monologue on the Dewey Decimal System which had both us and the librarians howling with laughter A year later, we got the same gig, same delay, and they asked for the monologue again. Not only had he not kept it, he couldn't remember having done it. That's why it does not appear in the list. What a shame.

The thing about Johnny is that he's composed so much that you don't hear any one item very often. So it's been one of the joys of compiling this book to come across some real gems for the first time. One title that caught my eye was ***I've Got a Little Cottage in the Country.*** It could have been a soppy one says I. Not a bit of it. It is not a paean of domestic bliss, but a social comment on rich incomers depriving villagers of a roof over their heads. He can talk posh when he needs to, taking the mickey out of them talking about joining the "Lenguage Society" to understand the dialect. He rarely has a go at people with such comic venom. There is indeed a Northumbrian Language Society (notice, not "dialect") which is very active indeed, and every September they have a talk in Morpeth Town Hall. I dare say these are often quite earnest, or serious affairs. But in 2016, it was Johnny's turn to deliver. Not earnest or serious, needless to say, and very musical, since he's spent a career singing and writing in the dialect. For me, the highlight was his delivery of *Little Cottage.* It isn't possible to do justice to this on paper, but suffice it to say the decibel level of laughter after each punch line was "up a height" as they say up here.

The Great Australian Dancer. On the second Ranters Australian tour in 1981, we met a woman who had written a book comparing Australian and British dancers and styles of the participants. The cover of the book had a photograph of a man who could not dance, but had "The hat, the leather waistcoat, the beard, the hobnail boots and the tankard, and who created havoc at ceilidhs. He just wanted to be amongst it". He turned up at one of our ceilidhs down under, and completely wrecked the whole dance. "Every set he was in started to break up, and unfortunately it was a progressive dance, so the whole floor started to disintegrate. That's how the poem came about".

This reminds me of yet another of this man's talents. Not only was he central to any band he was in, he could if needed call for the dance. We were in Canberra doing a ceilidh on the same day as Charles and Diana's wedding, July 1982. He rose to the occasion by inventing a new dance. His main aim in this was to have sets rotating in circles like the spokes of a wheel. I do remember the success of this dance, even though the turnout was disappointing, the whole Ozzie population being engrossed with the wedding on TV.

Thoughtful

Many of his recitations tend to be thoughtful rather than comic. As he says "You can get a bit of dignity going, and it's not always easy to put a tune to an idea." Some of his songs were written for his children. **Matty** is a recitation for his youngest son, one with a chorus as good as you'll get from any poet:

> Matty is a good bairn, a canny bairn
> A rowley, powley, cuddly bairn
> But aa should've called him Jesus

Who else would have come up with that final line?

The Hang Glider and the Shepherd was composed after doing Tony Rose's club in Dorset in 1983. He was parked somewhere in the countryside, on a hillside with a beautiful view, when along comes a shepherd, unusually with a large Old English sheepdog. A little later there arrived a mini car with hang gliding gear on the roof. The shepherd stood resting on his stick, staring in amazement as they assembled the glider. They talked him through what they were doing, and suggested that he could have a go. He declined, but the whole scene, with juxtaposition of old and new, inspired our man to the composition. Another "sheep story" is ***The January Lamb.*** According to him, Leicester sheep are big, tough, very valuable in cross breeding, and being hardy, tend to lamb early. He heard the bleating of a lamb early in January, which to him seemed unusual. His take on this was quite philosophical. The poem reflects his maxim "New year new life".

It is notable that some of his best compositions involve shepherding, or other aspects of rural life. When at Bardon Mill, keeping multiple kinds of poultry, he noticed that mother duck had hatched lots of her eggs, and was duly looking after them. Unfortunately, the very last one was having difficulty in breaking out of the egg and was being ignored by the mother. Its beak just sticking out, Johnny took pity on it, and

Wor Johnny teks forst prize fer taakin', like

Michael Brown
Reporter
m.brown@ncjmedia.co.uk

A FORMER miner has made it a hat-trick of success for Northumbria's threatened dialect with his "canny" tale of a threatened Gateshead pit.

Retired teacher Johnny Handle has been crowned this year's National Dialect Champion after performing his poem Old Man Of The Village for judges.

After seeing off competition from Cumbria, Yorkshire, Lancashire, Lincolnshire, Devon, Cornwall and the Black Country, the 79-year-old, from High Spen, said the win very much proved that "shy bairns get nowt".

"I was absolutely gobsmacked when my name was announced as the winner of this cup because there were so many other strong performances from all over the country," said Mr Handle. "I never thought I had a chance."

His success at National Dialect Day, this year was hosted by the Lakeland Dialect Society at Rydal Hall in Cumbria, means that the Bill o' Bowes Cup has been won by members of the Northumbrian Language Society for the past three years, after Bob Bolam took home the prize in 2012 and Peter Arnold last year.

The society also won the Far Welter'd Trophy for the best group performance at the event's evening "Hentertyainment" concert.

"I learnt the dialect because I've lived here all my life and perhaps I picked it up stronger as I worked in the pits for 13 years, first at Throckley, then all the way along to Montague, Walbottle, Rising Sun and Ellington, before becoming a school

> Johnny Handle, of High Spen, who won national dialect competition-

demolition notice – on the village, as if there was no coal then what was the point of allowing it to survive? Obviously, it was not popular with the locals, who were fighting against it.

times the money was good and sometimes it was bad, and sometimes it was dirty and dusty, and sometimes you'd have a clean break and could almost eat your dinner off the seam – and celebrating the links

But the future for the Northu an dialect itself is less certain, number of people who speak it dies.

"It's an uphill battle becau today have their own diale

Johnny wins the national dialect competition

started to help it break free. "It came out in my hands. I felt I was its midwife. I gave it to its mother and she took it up." An event deserving a poem of course and ***The Odd'n*** was the result. (Not to be confused with the pit song *Runnin for the odd'n*)

Two other poems which are rather wistful inspirations from nature are ***Kestrel***, concentrating on the raptor's increased presence on motorway verges, and ***Valentine Dance*** composed after watching two leaves dancing around each other in the wind.

For a number of years, a gang of North East folkies led by The Keelers rounded off a somewhat vigorous festive programme of festive events with a singing session at lunchtime on New Year's Day. The location was the front bar of what was then a wonderful old fashioned pub right under Byker Bridge. Johnny and Chris always came. The event was duly held on 1ˢᵗ January 2000, and Johnny felt the occasion warranted a poem. Accordingly, **In 2000 Years** was first performed at The Ship at Byker on the first day of the new millennium.

As we have seen, when living at Bardon Mill he took a great interest in local events and people. Having been invited to do a gig at and Allendale Cricket Club prizegiving, he did extensive research and produced a monologue called **Allendale Won the Cup**. On the day, the men featured in the recitation were so drunk they weren't listening. Afterwords they said "Oh Johnny is tharaboot us? Ee lad, I'm sorry. Will you sing it again, I'll get order."

Events remembered

For no apparent reason in the year 2000, he remembered two characters from his days in the pits in the sixties. **Jimmy Doon the Shaft** recalls the man at East Walbottle in charge of the explosives, who enjoyed playing games with new recruits. "I was a bit green, and he used to throw me sticks of explosive to catch. Of course they don't go off without a detonator. Aa was havin a bit crack wi him, an' he says he's 'getting used to it now' so I asked him what he meant." Jimmy had been put on easy duties after the cage overshot and went up too high as Jimmy was due to push an empty tub into the cage. The tub, of course, went straight down the shaft, followed by Jimmy. It sounds awful, but following the great clouds of dust, rescuers being sent for, the manager was roused from his slumbers. Jimmy started climbing up the buntins, which were very slimy ("buntins" means a wooden framework which lined the shaft). He crawled out of the side of the shaft, and was in a right state. His marra, who was a religious man, saw him in his green slime, and thought it was his ghost. He ran straight to church in a terrified state and started praying for him. He wouldn't be told that Jimmy had survived. **Te Hear Aad Davey Talk** is about a pit deputy at Dudley, who dabbled in amateur dramatics, and was quite the orator. Men would want to hear him speak on almost any topic. After a heart attack he was put on "light duties" at the timber yard. "Kept the books and that. Toward the end of the day, when everything was sorted out and they'd nowt else to do, the men would get Davey to give them a story. (They used to do it doon the pit at bait time)". There'd be twenty men sitting around the stack of props and planks, with Davey on a bit of a platform. Pointing to a worker's lunch bag, he'd do a bit of Shakespeare then drop into the vernacular, 'Is that thy handbarg there aa see?' In the Appendix to this book, Johnny includes these two recitations in his vivid description of life in the Dudley area when working in the pits. **Wallsend Explosion** was composed as a poem to complement a project on "Coal and Shipyards" in the North Tyneside Junior Schools.

Others

Come to the Briny Ocean is a tongue in cheek exposition of the delights of a trip to the North East coast, written for the *North Sea Suite*.

> Come to the briny ocean
> Get your frozen toes in motion

Sheer poetry. Or, as Louis used to shout, "Doggerel!"

A notable event in recent years was the Gateshead Garden Festival in 1990. These festivals moved around the country, concentrating on recovering industrial land in inner cities, and putting on a festival which would set up an enduring legacy. Gateshead's was particularly successful in these respects, and there was a lot of money sloshing about for entertainment for the two weeks that it ran. Being Tyneside, folk musicians did very well out of it, and one of Johnny's jobs was compering the Main Stage. One of the turns was a lady who was a red-hot flower arranger, so good that she qualified for a recitation, **Flower Arranging,** which she was so impressed with that she used it to advertise her shows.

Cat up a Tree arose when the neighbour's cat at High Spen took up residence in a tree, on a branch which had previously been a regular perch of a local tawny owl. The poem describes somewhat fancifully how the cat sat there thinking it was an owl, and wanted to try flying.

Other composers' recitations

Since starting composing in the late fifties, Johnny's gigs have either featured traditional North East songs or his own. He has not in general done any songs of contemporary songwriters. However, when it comes to recitations, the story is a different one. On seeing Johnny, Tommy, and Louis on various gigs in the sixties, anotable feature I hadn't seen elsewhere were local versions of famous bible stories. These apparently arose in the parallel cultures of Scott Dobson's *Larn yersel' Geordie* books and *Geordierama*, a stage act and LP by Mike Neville and George House, both local BBC Announcers. Johnny tells me that he, Louis, Tom, Jim Irvine, and others took on *Moses* and *Christmas* as standards in their gigs, and added some extra bits. He also started doing *Water into Wine*, *David and Goliath*, and *The Battle of Jericho*. He reports a demand at some folk clubs, particularly the Seven Stars at Ponteland, for him to do a different one each time he was booked. Others he recalls were *The Frogs*, and *Ghengis Sprott, Infidel of the Byres*. He says he doesn't know whether he could remember the stories now, but when challenged he admits to Ghengis, saying only that "It hefts well on the gob". A showman of the first water! Sidmouth Folk Festival once had a morning of Bible stories in the Beach Hut, with some from other parts of the country, but Tom and Johnny had the longest ones. These were recorded by the EFDSS and stored in the sound library at Cecil Sharp House, but when he called in, while gigging in London once, he found they had disappeared.

One monologue I've often seen him doing is *The Tyneside Tatooist*, where he's the little man faced with the task of tattooing the whole of a somewhat voluptuous lady ("She was gorgeous, but enormous..."). Even thinking about it as I write, I start to giggle. The subject is perfectly suited to Johnny of course, and his delivery is masterful. There was a headmaster from South Shields, Alex Forrester, big in the South Shields Amateur Operatic Society, who regularly did comedy routines, who made a recording in the early fifties, and Johnny got it off the record. However, Alex later told him that it was written by a mate of his from the society, and that there is a room named after him in Shields Theatre.

One of the best monologues written during the revival is Ed Pickford's *The Darts Match (Uncle Albert's Heroic Farewell)*, containing the immortal couplet

Twas the year of the first Yankee moonmen
(There was racing from Catt'rick as well)

It's a hard one to resist, and many Tyneside performers have done it, notably Tom Gilfellon and Jim Mageean, but I've never heard Johnny do it. However, in recent times, he has dedicated whole CDs to two composers, one from the past and one still writing. Billy Bell was a roadman working for the council in north Northumberland, who created over 300 poems commenting on the changing times in the northernmost part of England. He was at his most active in Edwardian days, and as Johnny points out in his notes to the CD, he had in his lifetime witnessed the coming of the railways, traction engines, cycles, cars, and the building of the Catcleugh Reservoir. His ideas were gleaned from travellers he met in the course of his duties, mainly on the A68 between Byrness and Carter Bar. Johnny recorded a selection of eighteen of Billy's poems, with a couple set to music and accompanied on accordion, interspersed with dance tunes. Whilst a lot of them were new to me, a couple have been heard frequently during my time up here since the mid-seventies. The Bellingham Show, held in August, is very big in the far north, and no less than three people have felt inspired to write songs or monologues about the day. Billy's immortal **Bellingham Show** recounts the visit of a naïve farmer who gets taken for all he's got by a "fly country jade". ("Which are the duck's eggs and which are the drakes? There's intelligent people at the Bellingham Show"). I've heard Johnny do it many times, but it never palls. The other is *The Dosin' of the Hoggs*, which is about sheep dipping, and generally sung to a tune of Jimmy White's. The range of the poems, from comical to quite profound, I feel reflects the range of Johnny's own compositions. In fact, had he been born in the 1800s, he could well have been Billy Bell.

The other CD is a selection of the monologues of Gary Hogg, a man very much of our time. With a background in folk clubs, particularly Cramington, he is a monologuist extraordinaire, with a particular affection for the Lancashire ones created by Marriott Edgar and performed by Stanley Holloway. Bernard Wrigley (The Bolton bullfrog) and comic Bill Maynard, have each recorded many of Gary's creations. Johnny, also an admirer of this genre, bit off Gary's hand when approached about recording some of his compositions. No, he wasn't bothered about finance, he just wanted to do them. Producer Kari Jones says Johnny was "a dream to work with making the CD, almost all done in one take, but when needed, he could pick it up in the middle of a track." Many of the classical monologues are done with piano accompaniment, and Johnny added accompaniment to the tracks. Meat and drink to him, of course, endlessly inventive, with nuggets like *Doggy in the window* inserted effortlessly. Although impressed with Johnny's approach to the recording, Gary comments that the launch event was "a nightmare", never knowing what the man would do next. Kind of sums him up! What is interesting is that these creations are described as comic monologues from the "North of England". I think that Gary is unusual for a Geordie in extending the "North" south of the Tees. For me, as a Lancastrian, the North starts at a line drawn between the Humber and the Mersey, and Gary's monologues are generic in this regard. That is why Bernard Wrigley, the "Bolton Bullfrog" with the most perfect of Lancashire accents, and the quintessential Geordie that is Johnny find them so easy and enjoyable to perform.

Chapter 9 The Tunes

"All roads to Whitby"

BY 1975 JOHNNY HAD COMPOSED AN IMPRESSIVE 33 SONGS, INCLUDING SOME of his best. However, despite being a consummate musician, as exemplified by his jazz days, and a great deal of Northumbrian tunes in the Ranters' repertoire, he had composed a mere four tunes. Maybe he was, after all, a bit modest about some things! However, since then he has been even more prolific with tunes than with songs, having no less than 317 to date. The bulk of these have been composed since the 1980s. Here is a breakdown of the numbers by decade:

1960s	4
1970s	4
1980s	34 (15 in 89)
1990s	104
2000s	154
2010-2012	9

As with the songs I have carried out a selection, hopefully representative of the genre. The "antidote" to the folksong book was his 1992 book of tunes, *The Johnny Handle Manuscripts Volume One*. I've not seen any successors, but the front covers of songbook and tunebook speak volumes. The early songbook shows a young man, bursting with life, in a sheepskin jacket, whereas the tunebook has a middle aged man, wearing a tie and glasses, sitting at a desk poised with a pen over a piece of manuscript paper. This was a new Johnny! Having already used traditional tunes to accompany dances, and songs in his concerts, he composed tunes in the similar categories of air, waltz, hornpipe, strathspey, march, rant, jig, and reel, together with ragtime items from his jazz days. He was also conscious of the mechanics of instruments, which helped him

Illustration for Braunston Locks by Johnny

to develop phrasing which suited them, and was able to offer suitable melodies to performers to try out. He has composed tunes for his six children: Susan *My December Rose* 2000, Ian *The Galloping Plumber* 1990, Anna *Miss Anna Pandrich of Carrsgate* 1988, Jonathan *Bouncing Jonathan*, 1988, Matthew, *Mealy the Mouse* 1989, and Megan *Baby in the Bath* 1986 and *Lass Divvent Grow Up* 1990. Other melodies are often for or about people from grandchildren to musicians, or friends.

Several tunes arc dance tunes in keeping with national and local tradition, including *Moonshine Polka*, *The Blackberry Bank* (hornpipe), *The Pine Grove Waltz* and *Braunston Locks* (jig or march). All of these are excellent tunes, having much more drive than most other tunes of their ilk. Flavours of syncopation creep in on occasions in his work. One, *Malvern Swings* is a rag, but a couple of his hornpipes, *The Fiddler's Stepladder*, and *The Difficult Fish* certainly swing more than most hornpipes. In more reflective mode, he is also very good at slow airs. Examples are *The Beech Tree*, and *The Wind on the Fell*. Most of the tunes just mentioned were created in the eighties.

His tune titles often reflect his personal experiences, from gigs, or meeting people. The former gave rise to *Blackberry Bank,* which commemorates a local gig at Bardon Mill for the Womens' Institute, *The Difficult Fish* describes a story from a meeting with a fly fisherman in a pub. On the road, *Braunston Locks* describes life on the midlands canals, and *All Roads to Whitby* (1999) reflects his passion for both the town and the incomparable Whitby Folk Week, still going strongly after 50-odd years.

As with his other compositions, many of his tunes have interesting stories attached to them. His first, **The Road to Ellington** was composed in 1962. He'd just returned from his stint at ICI Teesside and had a job back in the pits in Ellington, near Ashington in south east Northumberland, well outside the town where he was based. He comments on the road to the job, which was fine on the way to Ashington, until the turn to Ellington. He was in his notorious Bond Minicar (3-wheeler, central front wheel), and suddenly came across some serious subsidence on this evidently minor road. Hence his first tune. [Ashington was the "capital" of Northumberland mining, with its own dialect and culture, still mocked by Geordies. Ellington Colliery was the very last pit to close in the North East coalfield, as late as 2005].

Let us move to 1978 with **The Moonshine Polka**, composed on a trip to Norway with Colin Ross, doing schools in a country area in the north of the country. The problem they met with was the price of beer, about ten times the Newcastle price. With the schools closing at two o'clock, the evening yawned ahead of them, and then there were the weekends. This had a couple of useful outcome with the two of them them learning some Norwegian, and Johnny learning how to write out music from Colin. Then they met a Norwegian farmer, who invited them to play for his daughter's eighteenth birthday celebration, where they were served with some definitely illegal moonshine. (Apparently the local chemist, who provided the basic kit for brewing beer, which was legal, would ask quietly if they also needed some "whisky essence".) Despite the locals' seeming innocence, they were all in on the racket, a quieter version of the prohibition era in the States. The polka was composed in honour of the blessed relief enjoyed particularly by Johnny. He noticed later that it started with the same run of notes as the widely known *Primrose Polka*.

After telling me the moonshine story, he was reminded of another country with expensive beer, Denmark. The Ranters were doing a concert with Ali Bain and others, where there were crates of free beer. The next day, he would get the round in, but found he hadn't much money. Have you noticed how much more spontaneously generous he is than the average folk musician? As with Norway earlier, he would just have to lock himself in the hotel, to keep away from it. There was a band playing in the square next door to the hotel, he'd a half bottle of whisky, so emulated these bands and wrote a twiddly continental item, **The Skagen Waltz.**

A lot of his tunes came about when living at Bardon Mill, and he naturally got involved with the local people, as we have seen in the two previous chapters. But sometimes tunes arose, rather than songs. **The Blackberry Bank** is a hornpipe with a bit of a story. "When ye gan ootbye, it's amazing the strength of the WI (Women's Institute), and they were very active in getting local people to give them talks or performances. Any incomers with owt to offer were seized upon. So along I went to the Temperance Hall at Henshaw. It was full, with people from surrounding places like Halty, Haydon Bridge and Slaggyford." I am amazed he has resisted composing something about the last named place. "Anyway, I thought I'd just do my turn and away to the pub, but oh no, I had to judge the home-made wine. Right, I set briskly about it, sorted out two equal firsts, two equal runners-up, and a 'highly recommended' so as no one would be vexed. Then I'd be away to the pub." "Oh no, Johnny, you've hardly tasted them. Have some more!" They started loading him with large samples, which he of course could not refuse. "It was beautiful" says he. Needless to say, he wasn't going to make the pub at all, so these two women walked him home, holding him up, and dumping him unceremoniously at the door. Next day he met them again and asked about the wine. They told him about a special "Blackberry Bank", a stream coming down from the Roman Wall. He went there, picked the brambles, and made wine. And of course, wrote the tune. He did the do the next year, played the tune, and got lots of other WI gigs on the strength of it, for years and years.

The Difficult Fish is about a local man, a regular at the *Manor House Hotel* in Haltwhistle, a man with only one eye, who had difficulty with reading, which he needed for his job, and Johnny helped him out. The man was a champion fisherman, and had caught the biggest salmon on that stretch of the Tyne. He was casting with two different flies, caught the salmon with one, but the other caught on a bush, snagged and took his eye out. "Mind, I got the salmon" says he. And he was well pleased with the tune.

In his day job at school, he was pestered, along with many teachers, to go on a course. Apart from cynicism amongst teachers about these things, Johnny was genuinely concerned that a week without him would reverse all the progress he had made with the kids. Eventually he cracked, and picked a course where he would get the most out of it, one for peripatetic music teachers. It was at Malvern, where many locals were retired colonels with silent Rolls-Royces, contrasting sharply with the people on the course, who let us say were "A bit out of the norm" There were quite a few jazzers amongst them, and they of course would have jamming sessions. That's when he composed **Malvern Swings**, of course.

Some of the boys he taught at a later appointment which was a residential school were very tough, and would go for the teachers on occasion. He felt threatened a lot of the time, like "skating on thin ice", There was a place nearby where he could get to get away and calm down, a small copse of pine trees, which got its own tune, **The Pine Grove Waltz**, written about a peaceful wood near Stocksfield.

FORSTER CHARLTON AND HIS CAT — Air

A tribute to one of the best loved musicians in the North East. A great friend and a steadying influence in the heady days of the Folk Revival. 1990

One of my favourite tunes of his, which always brings out comments at music sessions is *Forster Charlton's Cat.* Forster we have met, as piper and fiddler at the Bridge and an early member of the Ranters. He was a batchelor who loved cooking and piping alike, and enjoyed throwing parties, especially for other musicians. He was a rather large man, and his cat was the feline equivalent, being well overfed by its master, and spent most of its time lying on the rather ancient couch "Like suet dumpling that's spread" awaiting its next meal. However, it was the only cat that enjoyed the Northumberland pipes. It would purr when they were played. (All other cats I know about would run a mile as soon as they hear the first note). Until I heard this story, I imagined a cat stalking about the house at midnight, gleefully surveying all it owned. In other words, stately but jaunty, chunky even. Maybe linked to being fed titbits? However, Johnny tells me that Forster enjoyed playing classical violin like Fritz Kreisler so he played it more legato. The power of music eh? This is what Johnny says in the Manuscripts: "A tribute to one of the best loved musicians in the North East. A great friend and steadying influence in the heady days of the folk revival. Another composition looking back on earlier days."

His leaving Bardon Mill was a major milestone in his life, but I had not heard **Farewell to Carrsgate** before. It's a very powerful lament, redolent of the grandest of Scottish airs, and definitely one of his best tunes.

Many of his compositions came about when he was on tour, with time to kill during the day of course. While practising some whistle airs for a booking near the New Forest, he was followed by a pony. This was the season when the animals gave birth, and as the pony lay contended beside him, he became anxious about his lack of vetinerary knowledge. However, once the new tune had been suitably composed, the pony ambled awkwardly away. **The New Forest Pony** and story went down well that night at the club. Written some years later, in celebration of the annual Whitby Folk Week which many of us have been attending since the late sixties, was **All Roads to Whitby**. For all northerners and many others it is the best folk event of the year. The same people come every year, punters and guests alike, and many have vowed to come to every Whitby till they die. The shepherds (Joe Hutton, Billy Atkinson, and Willy Taylor) now no longer with us, were told they'd got the gig till they died. There's a magic about the place even without the music. Coming from the north over the moors, with the heather in full bloom, you come over a rise a few miles out, and voila! The town is laid out before you like a map, with the Abbey, the Metropole, and the harbour prominent. Johnny feels as strongly about the place and the festival as me, and no doubt wrote the tune in 1999 with this in mind.

The tunes I have described have good reasons or stories attached to them, but they are also really good tunes. In the early nineties, I was playing with him and Chuck Fleming, and many of them have stuck in my repertoire. **The Fiddler's Stepladder** is one such tune, composed specifically for Chuck, allegedly on the fiddle. I am sure that's right, though I have never seen Johnny play the instrument, one of the few falling into this category.

Johnny is rightly famed for his other compositions, particularly the songs, but it is a shame that his tunes are not more widely played by other musicians. The few already described are but the tip of an iceberg of the tunes he has composed. So I looked through the list for eye-catching titles, and we had a session where he told the stories behind them, and later he recorded some of them for my benefit. Here are the notes he included with the recordings which shed light on his approach to the business of writing tunes:

"Compositions can take a long time to finish, sometimes years before I come back to them and try to find the right mindset. Others have to be made on the spot. I was playing solo for a birthday event in Cumberland in 1990 for the Cumberland Square Dance. I remembered the first two tunes in the set, but couldn't recall the third one. Loth to leave the sixty or so dancers rooted to the spot, I played on, making it up. Several people came up to me afterwards to ask what "the splendid tune was?" Thus **Jan's Birthday Jig** was born. This is a rough recording to give you an idea of the tunes. Some are polished and settled, others are just a bare framework, and have some (or no) potential. I improvise around the former and build up something. That suits me, but it always comes down to others' ears for any prolonged exploration e.g. gigs, presentations, historical concepts etc. Then there is the sheer "toying" element when you can experiment with melodies, harmonically, or variations on the basic structure e.g. rock 'n' roll, boogie, blues, beat or baroque approach."

It's funny how tunes, in particular, vary in their effect on the listener. Johnny sent me recordings of about twenty I didn't know, but most did not give me a "hit". They had either an interesting story, an interesting title, but by his standards, seemed ordinary. Well, it's inevitable isn't it? If we look back at the great Tyneside composers of yesteryear, JP Robson, Ned Corvan, Joe Wilson, and George Ridley, only a small fraction of their output is still sung today. So maybe Johnny, on perhaps the weakest of his compositional fronts, is on a par with these giants. In terms of his song survival, he surpasses all of these legends. Yes, we live in a faster, more intense age, with records, and folk clubs and festivals, but I just feel that maybe he has done better than the giants upon whose shoulders he has stood.

The tunes he sent me that I found really good included **Halty Satdy Morning** and **Halty Market Day**, both composed towards the end of his time at Bardon Mill, and complementing the songs discussed in Chapter 7. It is clear that Haltwhistle had a great effect on him. Other tunes he's mentioned to me include **Compliments to Scott Skinner**, the great 19th century composer, fiddler, and entertainer, a tune with many variations, which was a speciality of the great man. He thinks the best tune he ever wrote was a rag **Summer Sensation**, which seems not as good as the ones I described earlier in this chapter. Two tunes composed for old friends were **Septuagenarian Polka**, for Colin's seventieth birthday, and **The Gateshead Strut** for Louis. Whilst I cannot recall the tune, his description of **Here Comes the Coalman** sticks in the mind. "It's icy winter, the man has to park at top of the street and come all the way down slipping and sliding, when your coalhouse has enough coal for two hours. I could have given him a bottle of whisky".

As an indication of how things have changed over the years, here's the front covers of two of his publications:

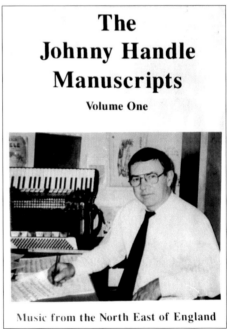

Chapter 10. To finish . . .

JOHNNY WAS NEARLY SIXTY WHEN HE AND CHRISTINE HENDRY MARRIED IN 1994, and a little later they moved out of town to High Spen, on the edge of Gateshead. Again he maintained his ties to the land. Life with Chris out there was busy, life was good, and though the gigs were getting fewer, he hardly noticed, still working with Gateshead as a part-time teacher. But eventually the innate entertainer emerged, looking for some outlet. So, a new era emerged as he started a successful series of bookings at old people's homes, Womens' Institutes, and similar places. He describes this period as "a canny gig for two hours". The first half he'd do Geordie stuff. Then he'd open the suitcase, hand out percussion instruments, and strike up with *MacNamara's band*. Followed by *Oh I do like to be beside the seaside, Scotland the Brave*, then American stuff like *Swannee River*, and *She'll be coming round the mountains*. A few more Geordie songs, then he'd remind them of their young Bradford Barn days with *Oh you beautiful doll, If you were the only girl,* and finish up with *I'll be your sweetheart*. He comments on the old people's homes: "They were different, and in the afternoon. Stories about these places I could just go on and on. You'd run out of tape." One story will suffice. He was out at one old folks' home, in Deckham, Gateshead, giving a jazzy rendering of *Whistling Rufus* with the residents giving full volume on cymbals, castanets, and drums behind him. Suddenly he saw a policeman "glowerin at us through window, and a little later he appeared at the lounge door. 'Caught at last I thought with a sinking feeling. Arrested for disturbing the peace.' Not a bit of it. He was the friendly neighbourhood officer, and he shouted above the din 'Have you got a spare tambourine for iss lad?'". There were maybe twenty places he toured regularly, nobody else was doing it, and he got to know the residents and the staff. He must have been a great hit. I wonder how many aging folkies could turn to that as a money earner, and also if you were anywhere else in the country, what would you have done instead of Geordie songs?

Johnny with produce

Handle with care

Another aspect of this "retirement" was that there were fewer opportunities for commercial recordings with nationally recognised companies, but he still had many ideas about songs, tunes and poems which he felt should be available. "I set about producing my own albums. Fortunately, I enlisted the help of Axis Audio at Haydon Bridge, Northumberland. Their brilliant recording engineer was Ren Hunter, who helped me in so many ways, not least with his patience when making several takes of difficult tracks". The arrangement meant he could just run off copies when the need arose, so it kept the costs down. In the previous chapter I talked about the tunes I'd learned from being in a group with him and Charlie Fleming. We recorded a tape cassette in 1992 called **Handle With Care.** Other CDs in this period included **A Good Line Of Patter** (airs and recitations), **Six Of The Best** (all new rags on the piano), **Down In Me Own Backyard** (the title song was described in Chapter 7), and no less than eight others [1]. This helped to keep his eye in with his own music. He continued to do solo gigs, but much fewer in number.

---

1   *The Collier Lad* (re-release of the 1975 album); *The Best of Johnny Handle; Old And New Geordie Songs For Kids; The Land Where The Fell Meets The Sky; Heather and Sweet Smoke* with Chris Hendry; *Fairly Truthful Tyneside Tales* (Gary Hogg monologues); *Billy Bell Redesdale Bard; Here dwells my Heart* with Chris Hendry.

Chris already had a reputation as one of Scotland's best women singers despite, like Ray Fisher, having lived most of her life in England. No doubt she and Johnny sang at home, but it was some years before they would do gigs together. When Johnny had a tour in Scotland, she would do a spot separately from him, then gradually he persuaded her to have accordion accompaniment. She had never had accompaniment at the Bridge in the old days, but she eventually preferred it to singing alone. He mentions a gig at Strometerry, in the remote West Highlands, singing in the bar, when the locals preferred to play pool. They were opposed to him interfering with the game, but when Chris stood up it was a different story. She took over the night. After that, says Johnny, "It just depended when gigs came up", but he started encouraging people to book the two of them. "It was a comfortable arrangement to work together and we complemented one another"

In musical ways, they at first appeared to the outsider to be incompatible. He the all-busking, unpredictable musician who had been loath to practise, she the staunchly traditional Scots singer, one of the greats, committed to accuracy in song. " I was nervous at first about whether I could fit in accordion accompaniments. Some of the more sensitive Scottish songs needed sympathetic handling. However it soon began to fit together. I enjoy the challenge of finding new things to work on. Having catalogued lots of material in my researches, it was easy to adopt the same working methods to our rehearsal. Getting older and playing less makes one worry about forgetting words, so we always plan our programmes carefully, with lyrics and arrangements to hand at our performances." Thus accordion accompaniments began to be used, as we worked on themes, arrangements and styles of delivery. The blending of our two repertoires produced a rich source of material. I composed some melodies for poems which particularly suited Chris's soaring voice, notably *The Mackerel Song*, *The Herd Laddie*, *Here Dwells my Heart*, and *Sally's Love for her Sailor*". There is no doubt that she has been a steadying influence, encouraging him to dig for more songs. She has certain keys – "A flat is tricky" says he. As Mike Tickell observed, "A new phase in his life".

And so say all of us. They did a gig at Tynefolk (the Blaydon folk club) in September 2016. They'd clearly planned the set list in detail, and had

Johnny and Chris (Photo by Andrew Day)

presumably practised long and hard. The first half started with a set of three rural songs and two of Johnny's tunes, including Chris's hilarious story of him getting attacked by a herd of cows up in Fife. The set ended with a set of two military songs and a comic Tyneside monologue new to everybody, I think, which he had unearthed from Allan's *Tyneside Songs* first edition of 1962. They started the second half, again with a themed set, this time located in the shipyards, once as important as mining in the North East. All four songs were contemporary, one of Archie Fisher's, one of Barrie Temple's, and two of Johnny's which he wrote in 1962 for the film *Sunderland Oak*. The rest of the evening was unthemed, but had tunes and songs reflecting his Tyneside roots, and Chris's Scots roots, though she finished with *Here dwells my heart* about the beauties of the Northumberland coast (tune by Johnny). An encore was inevitable after such a night, and the two of them sang the wonderful Scots song *Huntingtower* to finish.

This continuously evolving partnership has led to many appearances at clubs, concerts, and festivals. Their two CDs *Heather and Sweet Smoke,* and *Here Dwells my Heart* have been received with much acclaim, and a further collection is planned. Their reputation has led to travels around the British Isles from Cornwall to Aberdeen. In particular, he and Chris have been a double bill at Whitby for several years now, and they have been guests at several of the Scottish festivals, such as Stonehaven, Girvan, Falkland, and Cullerlie in the last two years. The last two places only book the finest of traditional singers. Cullerlie is given over to unaccompanied singing, which did not worry Johnny or Chris. Says Johnny "It was a fantastic weekend with the highest quality of singing." In 2009, they were invited to Australia, appearing at Gulgong Festival, held at an ex-gold mining town in the 'Outback', followed by work in Sydney. One of the highlights of their musical partnership was their concert at the Sage Gateshead in 2011, when Johnny was awarded the Gold Badge of the English Folk Dance and Song Society for services to North East folk culture. Johnny describes their approach to audiences as "Entertaining and informative, with a high standard of professionalism"

Yes, he still has appetite for new ideas. The Tyneside playwright Ed Waugh has just written a play about the nineteenth-century composer Ned Corvan, and needed to hear some of the songs. Vic Gammon recorded Johnny doing twenty of these, and was singularly impressed, given he'd not had time to practice, by his improvising accompaniment on the piano. The more so, since these were not in his normal repertoire. Alistair Anderson says they were both doing Dartmoor Festival in the same year (2015), and did a lot of playing together. "The quality of his voice is going down, so he's adjusted his style. He still tells the song really well, better than ever, with his conversational delivery." Then there's Carol Anderson, the prodigious Scots fiddle player he'd met at Whitby in 2014. Two years later she was trying to get a session away at the same festival, and in a quiet interlude there piped up an accordion player playing quietly from the back She instantly said to the crowd "Is that Johnny Handle?" Yes, it was him, and the tune was one he'd written about her two years earlier *The wee lassie with the long bow*.

He still gets commissions, as described in **Under the fields of Heaton** in Chapter 7. Mike Tickell says "As he gets older, he's starting to get into his main flow now. I was very impressed by the time and energy that went into the Whitby show, what with all the research, going way outbye to take photos [he's referring to a 2016 re-vamp of *The Tyne Valley Suite*

Johnny with the cast of the show at Hartlepool Folk Festival

described in Chapter 5.] Yes, says Mike, he's a grafter, but not a good delegator (apparently Johnny took over the technical side of the show, which Mike thought he was doing. Alas, the man is not perfect!)

At the revived Hartlepool Folk Festival in 2015, he presented a whole show about mining, with various folk luminaries, local people, and the Durham Miners' Association Brass Band. This was in St Hilda's Church on the Headland just out of town, with an amazing atmosphere, great sound, and lighting effects. A tricky job to get everything co-ordinated and the timing right. Nobody could have done it better, and with such a command of the subject.

In April 2017, I saw him do a smaller booking in Wylam in the Tyne Valley. The local film club were showing *The Miners' Hymns*, by the American Bill Morrison with music by the Icelandic composer Johann Johannsson which I'd not heard of, but is a masterpiece. I've seen a lot of "footage" of the North East coalfield in my time, but this was exceptional. Johnny preceded the film with a few well chosen mining songs, which went down really well with this audience of mainly non-mining folk. They loved his music and his patter borne of experience, and after the film made many positive comments about it. He can reach any audience with ease.

I hope that the book has established his credentials as musician, singer, composer, and entertainer in folk music. As already hinted, he could have kept with the jazz, but chose folk. I am a few years younger than him, and loved traditional jazz, which was played by people about 10 years older than me – they all seemed to wear corduroy jackets and cavalry twill trousers, so I got swayed by Fats Domino and Chuck Berry in the fifties, but thankfully also by American folk songs, courtesy largely of Lonnie Donegan. One fascinating thing in the story is "Why did he take the folk route?" He has not said much himself, except "Without folk I would have gone into blues, like Alan Price, but I never had the getup and go. Folk made more sense. I was looking for the right combination of musicians to work with, as King Oliver and Louis Armstrong had done in the Classic Jazz period of the twenties. I never lost my love of jazz. Jazz was inspirational, just like the Ranters. When we were playing together, we gelled." He claims it was Louis who persuaded him to take the folk route, which may have been the case, but I think there is more to it. He was clearly enjoying the jazz, but as we saw earlier when he discovered the local musical culture he took to it with enthusiasm, and saw its potential and that he could help develop it. He has been tremendously active in furthering the tradition, and in enhancing it by both his performance and creations. I believe that there is nowhere else in England that has had such a rich musical tradition, and have presented the evidence elsewhere[2]. Here is a brief summary.

Whilst we have a large number of English folksongs, which were collected around the turn of the nineteenth century mainly in the southern counties, nobody collected in the North East during that period. However, there had been collectors in the area well before that, such as Joseph Ritson and John Bell, who had found a number of songs in rural Northumberland of outstanding quality. Examples are *Bonny at morn, Dollia, Felton lonnin,* and *I drew my ship into a harbour.* They are like the folk songs later found in the south of England, but are different in several respects. They use local dialect, hardly any have been found anywhere else, and the tunes seem also to be unique to the area. They could be seen as "Local Folk Songs" for now. It is still the case that few

---

2   http://www.mustrad.org.uk/articles/ne_songs.htm; http://tynefolk.co.uk/folk-articles-geordie-singing.php; Pete Wood, *The Elliotts of Birtley, Chapter 6 "Singing Traditions"* Herron Publishing, 2008

of the southern songs have been found in the region, whereas they were widely distributed elsewhere in England. As well as songs, the NE has its own traditional tunes, many of which are unique to the area.

Whereas the local folk songs just described are anonymous, in common with other folk songs, the area is also distinguished by a huge number of songs whose composers are well known. Whilst the earliest of these date from early in the nineteenth century, the most active period was from the 1840s to the 1860s, when composers such as Ned Corvan and Joe Wilson, also performers in the flourishing music halls of Newcastle, left behind them a lasting song culture which has survived to this day. After this peak, there were other composers, such as Rowland Harrison and Tommy Armstrong, the latter taking this tradition into the start of the twentieth century. For the discussion, I will call them "composed songs".

How do we know about these two traditions? The answer may lie in the extensive musical publishing activity that has occurred, almost all of it in Newcastle. The collectors Ritson and Bell published in 1793 and 1812 respectively, and were succeeded by Collingwood Bruce and Stokoe towards the end of the century. All of these contained mostly the local folk songs. How about the composed songs? There were three ways in which they were published. Many composers would publish their own songs, but other people might also publish them. Newcastle had some of the most prolific broadside printers outside London. Thus Marshall, Angus, and Fordyce between them put out hundreds of songs, including many locally composed songs. Marshall in particular published many song books of local songs, and all three published many song chapbooks. These and other printers published more of these small booklets than anywhere else in England, London included, again including many of the local composed songs[3]. In fact, some of these, containing up to thirty songs, would be dedicated to one composer. Many of Ned Corvan's songs were printed in four chapbooks by Fordyce. One of the most important publications was Thomas Allen's *Tyneside Songs*, started in 1862, with a final edition in 1891. Allen included the 19th century composers and the local folk songs of the 18th

---

3   Wood, Peter Chapter 4 "The Newcastle Song Chapbooks" in *Street Ballads in Nineteenth-century Britain, Ireland, and North America* edited by Atkinson & Roud, Ashgate (2014)

century, with copious illustrations and biographies of the composers, giving a most useful flavour of the importance of these songs at the height of the industrial revolution.

We have looked at the very full 19th century Newcastle song publishing record, but none of these were available to ordinary working people, if only for financial reasons. The man who made the songs available was Catcheside Warrington (Catchy), who we met in Chapter 1. Thus it was that the young Johnny had heard these songs in the family nights during the war, and brother Brian recalls his father carefully removing the brown paper that catalogue parcels arrived wrapped in, and carefully preserving it to cover books (my father did the same-now we "recycle"). In the Pandrich household, such books included Catchy's. But in his early twenties, Johnny was more into jazz and skiffle than local stuff, and was established as a great jazz musician in several local bands. He saw the songs as music hall, accepted by people as "Geordie stuff" like the football. In schools they'd had the southern songs, collected by the likes of Vaughan Williams and Percy Grainger. When I pointed out the national popularity of Bobby Shaftoe and Keel Row, he says this was "fringe", the music hall stuff was seen as more relevant, established in his parents' generation by Catchy. *Wotcheor Geordie* was a BBC radio programme that ran during the forties and fifties. It featured a large number of variety performers such as the Barry sisters, the five Smith brothers, Jack Armstrong's band the Barnstormers, the Northumbrian Serenaders choir, and local comedians such as Bobbie Thompson. But it did include Billy Pigg, and songwriter Jack Robson. Despite this, Johnny felt it was a bit corny, presenting Geordies as clowns. For him, it lacked depth.

We perhaps need to remind ourselves that Catchy was the only source of songs easily available at that time. Such books as Allan's and *The Northumbrian Minstrelsy* would only be found in certain libraries and the odd second hand bookshop. What converted Johnny was a then recent book by Bert Lloyd, *Come All Ye Bold Miners*, as described in Chapter 3. It immediately interested him because he was working in the pits, and "The book made me think it was only the tip of the iceberg." Although he'd seen the names Corvan and Wilson, he didn't know much about them, but did write his first song, about a pit, as early as 1958. He now waxes lyrical about Joe Wilson, who "Alhough using domestic subjects, his songs revealed the social setup of the times".

It is interesting that he was slighting about *Whatcheor* when he went on to present himself as a bit of a comic, but we'll come round to that a little later. What is certain is that he would have had to do a lot of digging to find local songs that were pit-based. Meanwhile, the country was getting a picture of the North East via comedy, or what he calls "The Geordie Revival", which continued in the seventies with people like Scott Dobson, who published *Larn yersel' Geordie* in 1969, and followed that up with a string of similar booklets during the 1970s. So it was time to square the circle in terms of musical tradition, which Johnny spearheaded in the sixties, with support from some others who were beginning to realise that the area had something special to offer. Frank Graham started publishing local books in 1960, with his first books on the castles, battles and town histories of the area, along with a number on the social and military history of Hadrian's Wall. However, his publication of *Larn Yersel Geordie* was controversial. Some felt it just made a joke out of local dialect and culture. But it was also an extraordinary success: the first run of 3,000 copies sold out in 48 hours and a total of 81,000 copies were sold in the first year, making it possible for him to reprint Bell's *Rhymes* and Allan's *Tyneside Songs*, as well as new books such as Tom Gilfellon's book of Tommy Armstrong songs. Frank also kept works by local writers Sid Chaplin and Jack Common in print. When the firm was sold in 1987 it had published 387 titles (of which 103 were written by Frank himself) with total sales of over three million copies, a British record for local publishing. Sure, it was a period when all places were re-visiting their local cultures, but none, in my opinion, had such a wide range of musical styles to offer as Tyneside. Other large cities didn't have the material.

When I say to Johnny that the place is unique, he says it's "not quite the word". Let me say straightaway that he does not make this claim himself. Indeed, he is all-embracing in his love of other cultures. I think I've talked about my own area, Lancashire, earlier in this book. He picks up on such phrases as "tripe mines" and "Albert Murgatroyd" and other imagined Lancashire folk who would pepper his stories for years afterwards. (Harry Boardman seems to have been some sort of role model here.) He stresses that the song tradition was much weaker than the music tradition. "There is evidence that there had been songs, but it's a bit like dinosaurs – you know the bones are there, but where are the animals?" This is borne out by two national anthologies. *The folksongs of Britain* is a series of ten LPs featuring recordings of source singers from the British Isles, collected by Peter Kennedy, Alan Lomax and others in the late 1950s. It drew heavily on three regions, Ireland, Scotland, and the south of England. Out of about 500 items, only three songs came from the North East, from rural Northumberland. Later, well into the revival, a series of twenty CDs were issued by Topic Records, called *The Voice of the People*, again with about 500 items from source singers and musicians. This series had not a single song from the North East, but a whole album of music from the region. But from where I am sitting, the area teams with local songs, as outlined earlier in this chapter. Johnny concentrates on the period from about 1890 to the folk revival, saying "The songs were a narrow thread, following on from those four books [Catchy's. The Catcheside Warrington books described in Chapter 1]. The song tradition is only strong because of the revival. The Catchy songs were not classical, they were not folkie, but they were OUR songs. People [not just folkies] remembered maybe twenty five Geordie songs which were theirs." This puts me in mind of the Gustave Mahler quote "Tradition is not about worshipping the ashes, it's about tending the flame." The point I would wish to make at this point is that in Newcastle and the North East, there was a flame to be tended. It was different elsewhere, or to use Johnny's expression, at least there were bones! However, if he's right about the revival re-establishing a North East song culture, then he has undoubtedly led it. What features of his character have contributed to this achievement?

Let us turn to his musicianship. Earlier chapters have outlined more than twenty instruments that he can play, to varying levels of competence. He has a native curiosity to "have a go", to find out how an instrument works, to get a tune out of it, without ever having looked at a tutor for the thing. At this, he has been amazingly successful, to the extent that his prowess has become legendary. Dave Normanton tells this story: "Johnny went into a room, and there was a Scots piper there. Somebody who knew Johnny says "I'll bet you can't get a tune out of those. You may be able to handle the little ones." The piper says "If you can play a tune, you can have them." Johnny complied, played a tune, and took them away. To be fair to Dave he said "I might have got that wrong. It's what I heard. Best check it out." No" says Johnny, "Not quite. I was in the deep south and got an extra gig offered for £90. Using the extra money, I went to Hobgoblin, the London music shop, and offered to buy a set of pipes. As they were not made in Scotland, I insisted that the assistant, a melodeon player, played me a tune on them. Between him and me we managed *Amazing grace*. I already had a practice chanter, so knew the fingering. He blew and squeezed the bag, and held the drones up.in the end, to make the deal, after failing to control the whole beast." Well the truth is still good, but it shows how tales about this man can grow out of all proportion. As Ali Anderson observes "Give him a ham sandwich and he'll play a tune on it". Fellow Ranter Tom Gilfellon puts it another way: "Johnny is the most intuitive musician I've ever met in my life."

There is no doubt about his best instrument. On the piano he is supreme, playing the whole range of musical expression with consummate ease, all without passing a grade. Indeed, he was admonished for playing without the dots, and "went through three piano teachers" before he was ten. His is an exceptional natural talent which so many professional players of all genres would dearly love to have. Indeed, he went through his jazz phase, learning many instruments when his reading of music was limited, but showing great insight into chord structure and variety of accompaniment. We have seen how his reputation led to people giving him instruments, which often required "attention" before they were playable, meaning him learning repair techniques. He of course just loves doing this sort of thing. As we have seen, he loves going into technical detail about everything, especially geology and mining.

Of course, the phrase "Jack of all trades, master of none" may well be going through the reader's mind at this point, so let's look at this aspect. In his jazz days he was of course playing "ensemble", where he was at least competent on a wide range of instruments, both strings and brass. In his folk days, he was obliged to swap the melodeon for the accordion by popular consent among the residents at the club. The accordion, whilst not the most popular in English folk music, is the instrument he is mostly associated with, and which in his hands gives an immediate lift to whatever he is playing. As observed earlier, the combination of him and Colin Ross on the fiddle was a unique sound in the folk revival. This may be partially apocryphal, but I remember him going in for the competition at Newcastleton Gathering in the late seventies, taking several years before getting placed. God obviously loves a tryer! Actually, I believe him when he says he was being too imaginative with interpretation for the judges, who some very definite ideas how these Scots tunes should be played.

The other main feature of his success is his humour, of which several examples have been given in the book. His habit of calling non-folkie people as "humans" may often be seen as derisory, but equally has a truth within it, i.e. the folkies are obsessional about this particular genre to the exclusion of others. On stage, he can be zany, which often spills over into everyday life. Benny Graham told me this story: There we were at Rose Lea [Winlaton Mill] at teatime, when the phone rang as it always did at that time in those days. Johnny picks up the phone. "Hello, Hesperus Crint, Elephant Trainer". Puts the phone down. Two minutes later, phone rangs, he says the same thing. A third time, same thing. The fourth time he says to Benny "answer the phone". "Hello, Winlaton…." A nervous voices says "Is that where Johnny Handle lives?" "Ah" "Thank goodness for that. I've been talkin to a weird bloke who says he trains elephants" Now, I think the character is an invention of Johnny's, and comes up regularly in his conversation,but it wouldn't have happened without his early obsession with The Goons, which all happened at Heaton Grammar. He confesses to still using the same device for handling cold callers.

What else? He has a passion for the local tradition and folk music which he always wants to share with others. I talked about his approach to involving schoolchildren in musical projects at the end of Chapter 5. At festivals, particularly Whitby, people always approach him with something they want help with, often arising from his many workshops, and he takes a great deal of trouble to help them. Pete Coe, a great melodeon player amongst many other things told me that he got a great deal of help with Johnny in the early days of his playing the instrument. Although by his manner you'd think that he'd be "artistic" in organising his musical affairs, you would be wrong. Such a vast amount of material, both his own compositions and his research material needs a lot of management. He's got file after file with list after list, which have proved essential in helping me to write this book. Again, he pretends that he's not technical, but really he is. "Windows 10. It's got everything.", and handles *Sibelius* (the musical software) deftly. He wants to leave his legacy, with everything recorded and documented.

When I first came across him, in the sixties, I got the impression, like many others did, that he was a very talented showman, an entertainer a comedian. Sure the stuff he was doing was unusual, and authentic, but the man was too full of himself. I wouldn't then have been surprised had he gone way of comedians Connolly, Carrott, and Harding. Ed Pickford is the great thinker of the Northeast folk revival who hurries to let me know that he doesn't know him very well, has these things to say about Johnny: "He is the exemplar of 'I do therefore I am'. He could have taken a different track. People don't know the depths of his expertise as a musician, because he just presents the comedy. He is eccentric [it takes one to spot one]–pinning him down is difficult. He's a diamond, there's sparks off him. He's a firecracker, but what is he hiding? He's like an unexploded bomb, so talented he can't control it, doesn't know how to direct it, he needs to slow himself down. He's not engaging people, he has a barrier up-people are not allowed in." What Ed seems to be saying is that Johnny puts on an act.

But others who know him well think differently. Here's some of the things Benny Graham has to say: "Never has it been 'I cannot manage that', it's always been 'let's have a try'. He never makes a mess of it. When I ring him about a gig, he says 'I suppose this'll mean rehearsals'" When I comment to Benny that his knowledge of the songs is prodigious, Benny says "He doesn't go off at half cock. Before he stands on the stage, he always knows his stuff". Again, when I mention the EMI attempt to make him a national comedian, he emphasises the allotment stuff, and says: "Money doesn't drive him. What drives him is the creative process. It's all about the connectivity between the music and the area. I've seen him with a tear in his eye. It's his emotion about the place." I say "he's got it made, he can turn his hand to anything. He doesn't need to be a star." Benny says "I don't think he wants it." Yes, he wants to keep in contact with the earth, but also with his audience, as when he makes up a song going round the room making comments about the people listening, which many people have mentioned to me as magical, whereas both him and Eddie Pickford regard such talent as trivial. Maybe such creative people as these feel this way, but we mortals find it amazing. Vic Gammon says he's the supreme entertainer, and that he felt the need to act the clown because the rest of the Bridge were perhaps more formal in their presentation. But he agrees that there's more to him: "His songwriting is very good. *The old pubs* and *Guard yer man well* hit a chord. At his best he captures a certain moment of feeling that is really compelling. Not all songwriters manage that". He comments on him lecturing on the folk degree course-always lively, had good stuff to present, but almost couldn't get out of the joking mode, the self-parody, he was so used to doing.

Alistair Anderson says "His musical and great songwriting skills. would go down with the folk youngsters now very well. He draws the character of the Northeast, including caricatures, into what he's doing in ways that he can make work. It's sheer chutzpha and devilment. I think he has enjoyed creating tension, but has found it difficult to let go. But the man could always recover from the rough bits." Ali says he learnt stagecraft from him, but stresses that doesn't let his own solo audience get that uncomfortable! Another Ranter who mentioned this edginess in his performance was Tom Gilfellon, who describes a' big gig at Barrowlands in Glasgow with an audience that included the likes of Billy Connolly and Dick Gaughan, when Johnny, the worse for drink, started having a go at the Scots crowd. He obviously thought that this was the height of humour, but wound it up higher and higher. Tom felt the need to apologise and they beat a hasty retreat. This is probably another example of a tale growing in the telling. Mike Tickell describes the same aspect, agrees that his sparky humour sometimes goes too far. When teaching in Gateshead he met up with a prominent female councillor renowned for her zealous pursuance of political correctness. In characteristic form, he adopted "full-on Ashington mode", calling her "pet". She was so outraged that she wanted him disciplined. Mike, who was Education Advisor at the time, had to call upon his finest diplomatic skills to pour oil on the troubled waters. In the end, she said to Mike "It's all right pet"!!!

Picking up on Ali's comment about "the rough bits", I've rarely found him unable to handle a difficult situation, the nearest being this story. One time, after the second Australian tour, in 1982, the Ranters were booked on a Saturday night at Corstopitum Social Club. Now, the one place where a folk band would not get a gig is a social club. In the North

East industrial areas, such clubs where the men would spend a lot of their leisure time, were a huge business, mostly being supplied with very cheap beer by the Federation Brewery. A normal Saturday night would be bingo and ballroom dancing. The last thing that working people in the eighties wanted was folk music. However, this was not Ashington or Dunston, but Corbridge in the rural heartlands of Northumberland, and what is more, they wanted a ceilidh. Yes, what used to be called a barn dance-we'd take it on. They were advertising us as "famous Tyneside band, just back from their Australian tour." It all seemed very good, until we arrived there. This club, despite its location, was very big, with had three levels, all of which were choc-a-bloc with tables and chairs, mostly occupied. There was no floor space, and no dancing was expected. Johnny suddenly went pale, and said "we'll have to do our normal act We're bound to be paid off." (Throughout the club world, if you were not pleasing the audience, this would be your fate. Many a budding young singer or comic has felt suicidal after such a rejection). Well, we did the first set, about thirty minutes, doing the normal stuff. To say they were restless is to understate it. Most of them seemed reluctant to listen. We would be paid off, despite some particularly cringing patter from Johnny. But no. Up steps the concert chairman, a force in the land, and says: "Noo I wants a word wi ye all. These lads are very famous, so I want some order. They may not be everybody's cup of tea. They're certainly not mine. There's going to be better order." So we got a second spot, which I can't remember much about, but I do remember when the bingo was on, especially during something called "the snawbaal", the four of us huddled at the bar, and absolute, total silence. Anyway, Johnny worked very hard at the patter, and we got a third spot when we gave them *Cushy, Blaydon*, and *Keep your feet still* and got a quite positive reaction. We didn't get paid off, and Johnny has been using the phrase "my cup of tea" ever since.

Dave Normanton, who has worked off and on with Johnny for many years, says "The single word for him is 'unpredictable in every way' (he breaks into the Nat King Cole song *Unforgettable*). When he stands up we have no idea what he's going to do. Play accordion, piano, trumpet? Sing or recite? Sometimes I don't think he knows. But there is a switch. I've many a time said, without any warning: 'Johnny you're on now'. Bang! The switch is thrown. He's on the stage, gabbling away.

Afterwards, the switch is off. As an MC, I learnt a lot off Jim Irvine and Johnny. If you're in charge, you've got to be dominant, folk either love you or hate you." To emphasise Johnny in switched-off mode, he describes various Pandrich family dos, with his "big sisters" having him well under control. At brother Brian's wedding, mother insisted on John sitting next to her to "stop him misbehaving". There he sat with mouth shut. Says Dave "Me, I love him for his misbehaving." When I tell Dave the Corstopitum story, he says "He could have just held them. When he starts talking, he doesn't know what he's going to say himself. There's no script. In thirty or forty years, I've never seen him drunk, and I've never heard him use bad language. He respects his audience, builds a bridge with them. That's a Ken Dodd".

Several people have been inspired by him. Mike Tickell taped a radio programme in 1962, which included Johnny singing *The Collier Lad*. He knew songs from the North Tyne area, but for him it was a seminal moment. Although his father had been a miner, this was the first mining song he'd heard. "it seemed to free something up. His songwriting came from direct experience. He uses people and places just like the ballads. It is thus an old scene. I think a lot of the younger people could learn a lot from him." Gary Hogg mentions Eric Burdon's comment on Johnny in his biography (described in Chapter 2), and Luke Kelly, who was working as a porter in Newcastle, having no folk songs, but found The Bridge, came every week, "then went home and founded the Dubliners". [I'm not sure the last bit is technically true, but it would have seemed like that at the time]. At the same time, of course, his pioneering work in Newcastle inspired lots of people in the area to both start singing and set up their own folk clubs (described in Chapter 4).

An interesting person in the context of inspiration is Little Billy Fane, originally Malcolm Collins, ten years younger than Johnny, famous nationally as an actor in the TV series *Byker Grove* and the 2000 film *Billy Elliott*, and as a Geordie character and singer locally from his albums of Geordie songs and a regular column in the *Evening Chronicle*. He started off in folk clubs, had all the patter, which got longer and longer. Eventually he got too big for the folk clubs, but started to do concert parties in the social clubs. There is no doubt that he was inspired by Johnny, and even lodged with him at Winlaton Mill when he'd nowhere to live. "Yes" says Johnny, "he did my stuff. The joke was I would turn up at a club-'who'd ye have last week?', 'Fane', 'Oh that's me sunk'". Billy wanted to do Geordie stuff in the clubs, but Johnny told him "They don't want it-they want pop music and bingo, get drunk and forget the pits." He was right - Fane struggled at first. Says Johnny "Patter is what you need. You need to get them on your side." That's exactly what Billy did, and made a great success of it. Johnny had tried concert parties in the fifties, but had not been tempted to follow that route. Seems like it might have been easier than thrashing round the country doing hundreds of gigs a year, and earned him more money. Particularly since Billy maintained an interest in the local music with his own one-man shows on Wilson and Ridley, music hall nights at Balmbra's, then in later life doing probation and education work in more than sixty prisons. Johnny does not agree. He had appetite for what he has done, and is well content. As he says "I have met some great people in folk clubs. They are appreciative and hospitable. I have heard some great songs and music from all over the country. Many have become good friends."

Like others, I think he is a natural leader, a performer, an entertainer. But many people have pointed out his need to act the clown. Even Christine mentions this. " His doing throwaway songs was partly due to keeping the club night up, but also because he felt that he couldn't tackle difficult songs, i.e. do the songs justice. This continues to this day (she mentions the then imminent festival gigs in Scotland). These two aspects may well be related, of course. It seems he exudes confidence without it being there. But, as I hope this book has shown, there is a lot more to this man. The first time I heard this aspect of his character was on the radio ballad *The Big Hewer*, where he contributed some "actuality" as a miner: "The silence in the pit, it's like infinity, or the bottom of the ocean. It's peaceful, and yet it's sometimes frightening. You could be driven to panic with it, I think. You've never known absolute blackness, there's always stars and a moon. But there, there's nothing. And you can feel this pressing on you, the darkness." .These are not the comments of a jack the lad who's just seen there's pickings to be had in this folk scene. Other examples are to be found in the stories behind his compositions (Chapters 7 to 9). For instance, the tune *Valentine's dance*, and the poem that became a song *Goin to the mine*. As many have said, he has always been fearless on stage, never at a loss, usually doesn't cause offence (i.e. he gets away with rudeness by being a "cheeky chappy" as with

George Formby). But some of us have seen behind the mask, and when I approach him about nervousness, or lack of confidence, he talks about the present, being nervous about remembering his words or having to practice more on the accordion before a gig.

So, still going strong in his eighties, he has been central to the folk revival and certainly the place of the North East within it. His easy, accommodating manner has brought his music to the attention of many who would have otherwise passed it by. Yes, the area may have been blessed with more musical material than elsewhere, but to use his quote, you know the bones are there, but where are the animals? Well, he has dug the bones and provided the animals. He may have stood on the shoulders of the nineteenth century "Tyneside giants", such as Corvan and Wilson, but he has surely added far more than any of them by the depth and breadth of his musical activity.

Appendix

An article written by Johnny in 2010 for a local project describing his experiences working at Dudley Colliery.

On Bank(Surface)

I left Heaton Grammar School on March 6th 1952, and started at Dudley Colliery on March 16th, one day after my seventeenth birthday. After two years in the fifth form, due to being underage for the GCE exam, I found little attraction in year six. An interest in jazz and piano playing had taken over any academic longings, and I was ready to start work. My father was a school teacher and did not take this decision well, but he helped me to get signed on as a datal hand at Dudley Colliery, a seven mile cycle ride from Newcastle. We had already looked at the possibility of the Cambourne School of Mines in Cornwall, but fees were too dear. I agreed to pursue my studies on a part time basis, one day a week, funded by the NCB, at Ashington Technical College with the possibility of mine management. "As long as ye get passin' the exams, Aa'll se that ye get te dee aall the jobs, and gi' ye the time off", the Colliery Manager said to me at the brief interview (strange that a man in charge of 800 men, and a coal mine, should have such a broad accent, I thought, but later learnt that there was 'nee toffs' in this job).

A Grammar School education was not a suitable preparation for the shock that awaited me in the real world. However, I was reasonably fit, having spent much of my spare time camping, walking and youth hostelling around the North East. A fortnight's holiday before work turned out to be less attractive as I pursued my route (The Pennine Way) through driving rain and snow. The fells being too wet, it was mainly zigzagged through country roads and rough farm tracks, so that I was relieved when Haltwhistle eventually came into view through the mists. The warm train that took me back to Newcastle was a pleasant luxury.

Monday Morning. Standing in the Colliery Office waiting for instructions, rather self conscious in new blue 'too clean' overalls.

"Ye'll be gannin' the timmor yard", said the clerk, and pointed me past a row of single storey brick built buildings I later found out was "The Workshops". I found a circle of drably dressed old men looking with some reluctance at three large railway wagons. After introducing myself to them, the tallest said "Aa'm Jake, now th' day's a canny one for ye te try yersel oot. Just de what Aa tell ye and "Ye canna gan Wrang!" That phrase was to haunt me over the coming weeks. Joined by a lad of my own age, we then climbed up into the wagons, to unload their contents which were wooden pit props of various sizes. The method was to throw them into heaps, trying to assess their lengths as we went, and avoiding the men. They loaded them on to small trolleys known as "horney trams" to be pushed along a set of narrow rail lines to the 'Yard' - rows and rows of neatly stacked props, and 'Planks' (props sawn down the middle to give a flat edge) This exercise seemed to take for ever, and when it was finished, we moved to the next wagon, and then the next. By lunch time my arms and legs were aching.

I was continually asking everyone to repeat their comments as the broad dialect was hard to understand and quickly realised that I was to become the butt of their jokes over the next few weeks. I noticed that amongst the yard men there was a quieter member, who made fewer jibes, and seemed to me the 'Tally man', as he wrote down various things in a small notebook, and answered the phone in the small shed which stood by an open lift. This raised the trolleys piled with props to the heapstead, a building some twenty feet above us, where conveyors rattled and tubs ran in and out of the cages at the shaft. I later learnt that he was 'Aad Davie', an ex-deputy, who was on light work due to a heart condition.

As the first week progressed the loading and unloading of roof supports went further than just props, to include baulks of railway sleeper size, chocks (rectangular beechwood blocks), steel arches, metal straps and nine and ten foot steel joists. All stacked in neat piles, ready for the orders from underground as seam sizes and tunnel dimensions demanded. The ride home on my bike was often a slow and trying ordeal, but I have rarely slept so well after work. When the men (or lads, as they preferred to be known) found that I took their jibes about 'The Grammar School Kid' well enough, they became friendly and I was determined not to show any physical weakness. Jake would sometimes say "Divven't gan ower hard,

man, whey it up and tek it canny, then hinny man ye'll canna gan wrang".
The usual mission for a 'long stand' at the Blacksmiths, was followed by
being sent for my pay note a day early at the office, and an extra bucket
of coals for the 'steam' hoist. (It was worked by an electric motor!)

They would ask me about the Grammar School education, being
amazed to find that I knew nothing of industrial history, or the first world
war, the 1926 strike and the ensuing depression. After being initially shy
about their own experiences, they eventually responded to my questions,
and in the lulls amongst the work schedules I received a firsthand
education about these times. Two of the 'Lads' had been in the trenches
with a false leg and a single eye as evidence; All recalled living off the 'Co-
op note' (Loan) in the work-sparse days. Black legs were remembered
and named. The union also featured in these anecdotes with many tales
of kindness and support.

When timber yard orders were low, I was sent on other jobs around
the colliery yard., such as cleaning up spillage from the coal waggons
along the railway line, and throwing the shovelfulls of small coal above
my head into the trucks. How patient was the 'Owld Shifter', working
with me, when I missed and it went down his collar! I took an early lunch,
and relieved the stone pickers on the conveyors which carried the coals
from the shaft down to waiting trucks. I worked at the 'Landsale' where
coals were loaded from a hopper into coal merchants' bags for house
sales. In the Spring my name came up on the 'list' to go training for
underground work. For sixteen weeks I went to Bedlington each day to
the 'D' pit, near the station. Each intake comprised 120 boys from all over
south Northumberland. We occupied several huts to study first aid, and
principles of mine work. Part of the mine was a training gallery where
practical skills were taught. We learnt to set props, harness and control
ponies, and how wire rope haulage was used to transport coal tubs to the
shaft. Much emphasis was made about safety in the mine.

Every Tuesday afternoon we were part of teams digging out a low
stone heap, and loading the broken rock on to a chain conveyor leading
to twenty ton railway wagons. The round shovels had to be used both
right and left handed, but the trickiest part was the use of long handed
hammers (mells) to hit sharp chisels, splitting the large rocks along the
grain. I often thought it was rather like prisoners at Dartmoor Prison in
the quarries! One day I way waiting at the bus stop to go home, when one

of the trainees came over and said "De ye want te mek a few bob, keepin' toot?" I readily agreed, and was taken to the back of a nearby series of pit heaps where I watched for the 'pollis', as a dozen or so miners played pitch and toss. I received a welcome bonus for missing my bus! The whole course was a great contrast to the Grammar School tuition I had found so irksome, for it was learning with a practical and useful element. I studied enthusiastically, and for the only time in my life, came out as 'Top Student!! Returning to Dudley, it was disappointing to find that there were no underground positions available, so for another two months it was the usual surface work. One benefit around this time was the introduction of pit head baths (actually showers) which was welcomed by the village. One day, one of the 'Gaffers' spotted me idling and placed a small piece of paper in my hand, wrapped around a coin. "Tek that the barber's, now, and tell him it's from at the screens". The idea of an 'NCB barber' was new to me, but I quickly found out that the haircuts were done in a wood hut around the corner in the village, and that the barber was also the illegal bookmaker. Having completed this type of mission several times, I became the unofficial bookie's runner for the Pit Yard, and it was quite common to call in at the Workshops and even the Manager's office to collect bets, all small paper notes wrapped around sixpences, shillings, or even sometimes a half crown. If a horse did well, I sometimes received a reward of a few coins, which was a nice addition to my small pay. When the prop orders had all been sent down the pit, and new supplies neatly stacked in the timber yard, there was often a lull in work towards the end of the shift. The men would gather in the west part of the stacks, and sit and 'crack'. Mixed smells of pine logs, coal smoke and Condor Bar pipe baccy mingled in the summer afternoons. Occasionally the men would ask 'Owld Davie' to 'spoot'. If he was in the mood, he would step on a pile of props, or a tram, and recite. In his day he had been quite well known in the local drama groups. The news would spread around that 'Davie hes a mind te spoot', and quickly a few more workers would appear until a dozen or so made up his audience. He seemed to stick to the original lines of some Shakespeare or Wordsworth, until an improvisation would occur to him, which caused much merriment. "Is this a bait bag I see before thee?", or "Impale him with thy face shovel, Brutus". It was surprising, however, to see the respect paid to Davie by his listeners, listening to some of this rather highbrow stuff.

Te Hear Aad Davey talk, te hear Aad Davey talk,
He'd hev we spellboond in the the Yard,
Te hear Aad Davey talk.

Now Davey was a deppity, he worked at Dudley Pit,
He could test for gas and fire a shot,
Down the Yard Seam dry and hot,
Te keep a good flat was his lot,
Then at the kist he'd sit.

But when the belts were stopped, and bait time came around,
The lads wad sit there quiet,
Jam sandwiches their diet,
And nane could deny it,
Davey's patter was quite soond.

For Davey had been an actor, in a kinda local way,
He could mind the words sae well,
And at quotin' could excell,
Wondrous stories he wad tell,
If the lads said, "De away".

It didn't always happen, just if he was in the mood,
Then 'Hamlet' or 'Macbeth'
Ghosts, battles, life or death,
Until he paused for breath,
Man, they thowt that he was good.

Quotes..Is this a kist I see before me? When shall we three fillers meet
again? Dost thou carry thy bait in a handbag?

But Davey's heart got kinda weak, light work at bank for him,
And sometimes though it was quite hard,
He'd help oot in the timmer yard,
From work inbye he had been barred,
But life was not so grim.

For as the western sun sat low, when the shift's work was done,
Out there amang the timber piles,
The lads wad smoke and sit awhile,
Say'n, "Haaway, Davey, let's hear yer style,
Gan on let yer gob run".

Aa still remember, sittin' there, Aa thowt him such a sage,
The smell of condor bar and pine,
The days Aa worked at Dudley mine,
When whilin' oot till lowsin' time,
As Davey took the stage.

(from some fragments written in the 1950s, and finally put together in 2000!)

By now, I had a good idea of all the functions on the surface at a Colliery. There was movement of the tanky engines with their trails of wagons, full and empty over the 'Crossing' to mainline railways in the east; the cycle of coals flowing from the tubs , out of the cage, into the 'tipplers', down chutes to the screening belts, and down into the ever waiting waggons. Equipment and supports loading ready to go below; fitters, blacksmiths, joiners, lorries loading coal bags, and the movement of men about the place. Smoke from each building floated everywhere, and dust from the heap often mixed with the smell of engine oil, rust, and welding torches. There was a strong sense of community, the pit yard being only a short distance from the rows of houses which branched away, dependent on the activity. Each change of shift produced an outpouring of workers in and out of this coal machine of a place, so that it seemed that everyone was inexorably linked with the pit, and places like Newcastle seemed irrelevant (except for its football team). Due to the varied nature of the surface jobs I noticed how the pit looked after 'its own'. Injured workers were found suitable places to continue earning, and even those who were not the brightest members of village life had a job somewhere. Self important union men, shift supervisors, checkweighmen would hold their status carefully, and after a time I had a chance to work out 'pecking orders' to avoid offence or ridicule. I paid a shilling a week to the union. Even the old people of the village had their support in the system, with retired mineworkers' homes, free coal, and bags of logs from the pile of broken props and timber, which were sawed and bagged by the 'timmer yard lads'.

But the summer was soon over and a change was looming. One day, I was told to be ready to start below on the following week, and a new learning process was to begin.

Part Two. Underground

Entering the cage that Monday morning in October, after being searched for 'contraband' (cigarettes and matches), I nervously flicked my cap lamp around, noting how much bigger it was compared with the tub height cages at Bedlington, where we had to crouch on our 'Hunkers' while descending. The initial work for me below was concerned with helping to move the coal from the face to the shaft. Some days I would be fastening sets of tubs to wire ropes, other days using the small electric hoists to lower the tubs into position under the conveyor ends, as they poured out a continuous stream of coal. I was usually given tasks with older men, and they would point out various features of the tunnels as we walked towards our work places. "Thon's the Welsh Timmerin'; that's been there for thorty year and nivver budged" (a clever system of hexagonally arranged supports gave the feeling of being in a beehive). "This's where owld Bill was caught be the set and lost his leg, mind YE mek for the manhole, if ye hear it comin'". "There's ne need for props here, it gans through the whin, ye see." (an area of the tunnels unsupported due to the strength of the rock in a volcanic zone), and worst of all "They never got Tim oot o' there after the big faal, ye can sometimes hear his ghost wailin'"; This was to come back to me when I worked on my own at that particular bend and heard the strange sounds on a lonely foreshift.

A break from the coal transport work was getting my own pony, and transporting props on a 'horney tram' along a bendy tailgate to the coal face. For three weeks I got to know the pony well, and one day it saved me from a nasty accident by refusing to move past a part of the tunnel. After various attempts to cajole the beast into movement, I gave up and took a rest, pulling out my water bottle. There was a sudden creaking of rock and timber, and two yards ahead the roof fell in, with some rather nasty slabs of shale in the way. The pony's ears had been sharper than mine! Half an hour of clearing soon had the way clear, and the animal seemed to be grateful for the reward of some of my precious bait. At this time I found the disadvantage of a rolleywayman (rail layer) getting behind with his work. This meant as the face advanced, I had to do 'casts'; (throwing the props forward three or four times in the areas where there were no rails). For a while I was on the 'panels'. This meant being at the loading point where the coal face conveyor fed the tunnel conveyor, ready to switch it off in case of stoppage. I also had to throw any props and planks left by the timber lads over to the coal fillers as they shovelled away in the seam, but most important of all, manning the telephone, and imparting the success of dogs or horses as the results were relayed through the pit!

Whiling the time away I sometimes made up rhymes, for it was here I thought of '*The collier lad he's a canny lad, and he's always of good cheer, and he knaas how te work and he knaas how te shork, and he knaas how te sup good beer*'. As the fillers would sit on planks and props, having their bait, I used to pay them tunes on the mouth organ, missing odd notes due to coal dust in the reeds. Several times there was a panic on when the coal stopped and the overman would shout on the phone,"Haaway man, what's on? keep her gannin'", to which I would give the dreaded reply "Brokken belt" The face conveyor snapped if overloaded with too many stones, which sometimes fell from the roof. While working on the 'hambones' (clipping tubs on to an endless rope system), I caught my little finger in a chain link which partially severed the tendons and bones. The first aid team ran with me on a stretcher to the shaft, and in twelve minutes I had got to the surface into a waiting ambulance. One pit job in which they excelled.

The coldest job was at the shaft, where the main air stream entered the underground workings. On a cold December day you were frozen stiff pushing and shoving the tubs in and out of the cage. The joke for new starters here was to tell them that a "Pie Wife" came down on Friday lunchtimes with hot pies;,one I fell for only too easily, standing anxiously near the cold air to be first in the queue! A new change awaited me in March 1953. To get experience of the different underground jobs, lads were put on 'spare'. This meant hanging around in a group of ten or so old men and boys near a fierce looking 'master overman' who would dole out the various tasks in an incomprehensible pitmatic accent. He seemed permanently angry, and when he addressed me by name one day I was sure some unpleasant job had been selected. "It's yer borthda' th' day. De want the good news or the bad?" he grunted, much to the amusement of the onlookers. "Good", I said... " Ye can drink legal at the club now yer 18". "Bad", I said. "Foreshift Monda Twelve midneet" he intoned, and the crowd nodded sympathetically. From then on I worked alternative weeks in day shift 8am-4pm, and fore shift 12 midight-8am. Suddenly the mining cycle of shift work was upon me. A seven mile cycle ride in the dark winter evenings and dawns was not a pleasant prospect. The last bus from Newcastle got me to Dudley at 10.35, which meant hanging around the pit head till shift time. I used to huddle in the lamp cabin amongst the smell of oil, doing the homework for college. Noticing this, some of my fellow trainees who lived in the village mentioned it to their families, and I was invited, no, told, to "Get along te wor hoose in the Raas for a bite of supper and a warm afore ye gan doon." Such was the warm hearted generosity of these Dudley folk.

When we stood around Billy the Overman, waiting for jobs, there was considerable apprehension; the worst call for me was "Scrappin rails fra' the aad tailgit". This was a salvage job, recovering rails from an old tunnel. The snag was that the nearest rails to the access link drift had been removed, and the roof in this 30 yard section had reduced from 6 feet to 3 feet high. So two old men and myself had to trundle the rails on a horney tram for 400 yards, then they got me (as the young, fit one!!) to fasten a leather sling around my neck, and crawl along the last stretch, dragging the rails, one by one!! That was a long week. Foreshift was particularly bad on Mondays when the Sunday day/evening sleep was not long enough. Working on the panels at the face I was caught by the deputy sleeping.(a punishable offence in the pit). Unfortunately the main conveyor had stopped due to a derailment of tubs, but I had let the face conveyor continue, and was disappearing under a heap of coals. This caused me to make a song in later years called "*A tap on the heed in the Foreshift*". When the weather improved I did return to cycling but found myself sleeping in the verge at Gosforth Park on several occasions!

The dependency of the community on the mine and its continuing employment, led to a song called "*Going to the Mine*", which I put together after comparing the many different pit villages and the inevitability of boys following their fathers and brothers into working below. Eventually I found transport easier to a pit near Westerhope, North Walbottle, in May 1953, where I worked for a few weeks before becoming a Mine Surveyor, which was my main job until 1965. By then, although well qualified to take charge of the mine plans, there weren't enough pits to go round, so I took up teaching as a career. But the days amongst the mining folk still live strong in my memory, and it was an experience I was never to forget.

Johnny Handle 2010

Tuesdays at the Bridge 30-31
Tyne Tees TV 34, 55, 66, 85, 100
Tyne Valley Suite 66-68
Tynefolk 125

U

Uncle Billy 15
Uncle George 4-5, 15

V

Vieux Carreé band 11-12, 14
Voice of the people 133

W

Whitby Folk Week 44, 71, 97, 115, 119,
  135
White, Jimmy 73, 111
Wilson, Tony 56, 72-73, 75-76
Winlaton Mill 45, 47, 61, 93, 95, 135, 139
Wotcheor Geordie 131
Wrights bus 4